"In *I See You*, Terence Lester calls us back to the heart of our humanity and reminds readers that this heart was designed to beat for God and for neighbor. Lester has followed the Spirit into abandoned buildings, under highway bridges, and into homeless shelters to find community among forgotten and abandoned populations. His stirring narratives and powerful commentary reveal that homelessness is a symptom and a symbol of a nation entangled in greed, gentrification, arrogance, racism, and a sheer lack of consideration for all of its citizens. In a fashion that invokes the prophetic fire of Martin Luther King Jr. and the compassionate solidarity of Jesus Christ, Lester centralizes love as the key factor to dismantling evil and creating a more equal world."

Neichelle R. Guidry, Dean of the Chapel, Spelman College, creator, shepreaches

"When the Bible describes transformation, one of the central motifs is that of moving from blindness to sight. In *I See You*, Terence Lester serves as a spiritual guide of sorts, helping us to see critical arenas of life that are otherwise so easy to miss. Go on this journey with Terence—you will not be disappointed."

Daniel Hill, pastor, author of *White Awake*

"Terence Lester is a doer! This isn't a book about social theory or what we should do but rather this is a book about what has been done, is being done, and what is working. He speaks from his heart, a heart with experience in the trenches. Terence has been there. He knows what he is talking about, and he is doing something on a daily basis to address the needs of the most vulnerable in our country. This is a book by a servant leader who is leading a movement that is changing the world for many people. This is a love story. A love story for the most vulnerable and how love calls us to act. Love is an action word and Terence Lester is living love beyond walls. This is a must-read for anyone in ministry or who says they love the world that God died for."

Ralph Basui Watkins, The Peachtree Associate Professor of Evangelism and Church Growth, Columbia Theological Seminary, pastor of Wheat Street Baptist Church

"One of the conditions of truth is to allow the suffering to speak, which is why this book is the real talk, straight-no-chaser truth. Using personal narrative, theological conviction, and social analysis, Terence beautifully describes the misery that so many of our sisters and brothers in poverty face. After reading this book many will be inspired to live a more compassionate life rooted in faith, action, and love and will answer the call of the Spirit to do something to help heal our broken world. In this time of rampant social inequality and indifference to the plight of the poor, this book will comfort the afflicted and afflict the comfortable. But most of all it will invite us on a journey that will leave us saying, 'I see you.'"

Billy Michael Honor, public scholar, faith leader, and social justice organizer, *Huffington Post* contributor

"Terence Lester's writing in *I See You* is clearly inspired by life-changing experiences and Scripture. Each chapter seamlessly moves the reader from just receiving information to accepting an open invitation to become the hands and feet of our God and see the most vulnerable in our world. This book illuminates with such compassion what we already know—that suffering is not an isolated event that happens to 'them over there.' Suffering belongs to us as much as any other life experience. Each word I've read has changed me and challenged me. I pray you will allow *I See You* to do the same for you."

Casey J, Christian songwriter and storyteller

"Terence Lester's *I See You* is far more than an informative text on people experiencing homelessness. He aims and succeeds at humanizing people's experiences, and the featured narratives amplify a wide variety of human experiences. All the while, Lester encourages the reader to examine their biases and prejudices when it comes to people living in poverty and provides actionable steps and insights to change our way of thinking and support those in need."

Liz Kleinrock, diversity, equity, and inclusion coordinator at Citizens of the World Charter Schools

"As a person who has all the unfair privilege this world has to offer—I'm a white, straight, Christian man—I wish I had read Terence Lester's book *I See You* twenty years earlier. His unique ability to share the experiences of the most vulnerable among us through powerful narrative storytelling will grab the reader and pour into their hearts. The world needs more leaders like Terence Lester, and this book is a powerful example of how he will continue to change the world for the better."

Jeff Hilimire, chief executive officer of Dragon Army, cofounder of 48in48

"There are many men that talk about creating change, but there are few who actually do it. For years, Terence Lester has been putting in work on the ground. I'm excited we have another resource like *I See You* from him that's rooted in true on-the-ground research."

Sam Collier, national TV and radio host, speaker at North Point Ministries

"*I See You* is bursting with spirit and challenge. In clear and vulnerable prose, Terence truly shares his heart with us about the urgent call to love those who are impoverished. Privilege has a way of blinding us to the realities faced by those society has made invisible, and in true incarnational fashion, Terence takes us with him on a journey to uncover the true experiences of our most vulnerable neighbors. I pray folks will approach this book with a heart open to the call of Christ to love our neighbors as ourselves and with eyes open to see others for the divine image they inherently bear."

Chad Wright-Pittman, associate pastor of congregational care and community outreach, First Presbyterian Church, Anderson, SC

"With compassion and insight, Terence Lester leads us on a journey designed to free us from our fears and illuminate the simple but profound truth that the poor, the unhoused, are ultimately no different from anyone else. He reminds us that *homeless* is a set of circumstances, not an individual, and that we must jettison the stereotypes that shape our biases and embrace people experiencing homelessness for what they truly are: our neighbors—fellow human beings—who want to be safe, to be seen and respected, and to have opportunity. To read *I See You* is to be gently reminded that fear is the great divider. It keeps us from love, from seeing and opening our hearts. Terence's life and words reflect the powerful truth that we are woven together in the fabric of life and that every thread is precious."

Doniece Sandoval, founder, chief executive officer at Lava Mae

"Terence Lester uses his own humbling experiences and relationships to put faces and names to the challenges of homelessness and calls for accountability to overcome fear of the unknown. Readers are provoked to see the value that God has given to *every person* based solely on his image in which they've been created. *I See You* shines a light on the effect we can have collectively on poverty when we take action and reject fear of the unknown. This book is for those who are ready to boldly love those that society has taught us to fear."

Anna Ferguson, director of operations for REMERGE

"In this powerful testimony of the harsh realities of systemic poverty and homelessness, Terence Lester challenges us to care for the loose threads in the fabric of humanity as a way to heal the collective. Sharing his personal experiences, Lester walks us through the modern-day, informal caste system that has created a wide breach where hard-working families find themselves trapped despite working multiple jobs. Reading *I See You* made me feel connected to our brothers and sisters experiencing homelessness and encouraged me to do what I can to end the cycle of poverty."

Claudia Aguilar R., pastor for justice and witness, Virginia-Highland Church

"I loved reading *I See You.* Lester's voice shines through. He brings the reader on an amazing life journey to love those you encounter. For many years, I have admired his decision to live on the streets for some time and to be with the people who spend their days and nights dealing with the challenges of poverty. Lester helped me to understand more and to empathize more. He helped me to know a bit more about the stories of these wonderful people and friends. I particularly loved how he contrasted the emotions and feelings of fear versus love. 'There is a vast difference though between living with the fears that keep us safe and letting our fears control us and the actions we take, especially when it comes to the way we treat other people—like crossing the street when we see someone dressed differently.' This chapter was powerful for me and made me reflect on some of my own unfounded fears. Thank you!"

Bo Adams, chief learning and innovation officer, Mount Vernon Presbyterian School, executive director, Mount Vernon Institute for Innovation

"Terence Lester takes readers on an empathic and personal journey that requires all of us to evaluate how we see others. His willingness to step out of his comfort zone to endure the elements people are encountering daily is exemplary. Our homeless brothers and sisters are fighting for their lives, and this book requires readers to analyze if we will fight alongside them. I am confident that this book will bring the mind shift that is needed to turn apathy into empathy. Terence is not just telling stories; he is speaking life—one that he has experienced enough to champion."

Cornelius Lindsey, senior pastor at The Gathering Oasis Church

"If we are properly instructed and willing to take our blinders off, we can truly eradicate poverty and its debilitating effects on humanity. Terence Lester makes it impossible for the reader to remain on the sidelines in this fight. He passionately gives a face and a voice to those who have been lost in the margins of our selfish and material pursuits. *I See You* is more than an epiphany, it's a call to action we all must heed!"

Andre Landers, senior pastor, iThrive Christian Church

"With his remarkable gift of riveting storytelling, Terence Lester opens the eyes of our hearts, allowing us to see fellow image bearers of God who are often invisible and marginalized in our broken world. With skillful artistry, Lester paints a compassionate and compelling picture of the heart, hands, and feet of true neighborly love. *I See You* will not only open your eyes to the poor and the homeless but paradoxically you will also see your life in a new way."

Tom Nelson, author of *The Economics of Neighborly Love*

"Terence Lester challenges us to turn good intentions into action. *I See You* is a challenging, inspiring, and empowering book! With hard truths, a humble posture, and insights learned the hard way, Lester debunks the myths we have about poverty and homelessness and introduces us to the real people behind the statistics."

Nikki Toyama-Szeto, executive director, ESA/The Sider Center

"Howard Thurman said it is a 'strange freedom' to be seen and called by our name. Terence Lester invites us into this divine freedom in his challenging and inspiring book *I See You*. In his encouragement to us, we are reminded how each one matters and how love makes all the difference."

Mae Elise Cannon, author of *Social Justice Handbook* and *Just Spirituality*

TERENCE LESTER

FOREWORD BY DAVE GIBBONS

I SEE YOU

HOW LOVE OPENS OUR EYES TO INVISIBLE PEOPLE

An imprint of InterVarsity Press
Downers Grove, Illinois

InterVarsity Press
P.O. Box 1400, Downers Grove, IL 60515-1426
ivpress.com
email@ivpress.com

*InterVarsity Press® is the book-publishing division of InterVarsity Christian Fellowship/USA®, a movement
of students and faculty active on campus at hundreds of universities, colleges, and schools of nursing in the
United States of America, and a member movement of the International Fellowship of Evangelical Students.
For information about local and regional activities, visit intervarsity.org.*

*All Scripture quotations, unless otherwise indicated, are taken from The Holy Bible, New International
Version®, NIV®. Copyright © 1973, 1978, 1984, 2011 by Biblica, Inc.™ Used by permission of Zondervan.
All rights reserved worldwide. www.zondervan.com. The "NIV" and "New International Version" are
trademarks registered in the United States Patent and Trademark Office by Biblica, Inc.™*

*While any stories in this book are true, some names and identifying information may have been changed to
protect the privacy of individuals.*

*Published in association with the literary agency of D.C. Jacobson & Associates, an Author Management
Company. www.dcjacobson.com.*
Cover design and image composite: David Fassett
Interior design: Daniel van Loon
Images: blue and red abstract: © oxygen / Moment / Getty Images
black male portrait: © Maaike Glas / EyeEm / Getty Images
young woman portrait: © PhotoAlto/Frederic Cirou / Getty Images
Asian woman portrait: © Morsa Images / Digital Vision / Getty Images
male portrait: © Igor Ustynskyy / Moment / Getty Images

ISBN 978-0-8308-4572-9 (print)
ISBN 978-0-8308-6527-7 (digital)

Printed in the United States of America ∞

*InterVarsity Press is committed to ecological stewardship and to the conservation of natural resources
in all our operations. This book was printed using sustainably sourced paper.*

Library of Congress Cataloging-in-Publication Data
A catalog record for this book is available from the Library of Congress.

P	25	24	23	22	21	20	19	18	17	16	15	14	13	12	11	10	9	8	7	6	5	4	3	2	1
Y	37	36	35	34	33	32	31	30	29	28	27	26	25	24	23	22	21	20	19						

I dedicate this book to every child who has endured a day without a meal or clean drinking water; every homeless person overlooked, looked down on, or denied shelter; every person denied basic rights to health care; every person that has ever been affected by bad political policies; every person enduring gentrification because of greed and dismissiveness; every person working long hours with little pay and compounded hopelessness; and the billions of people wrestling with poverty nationally and globally.

May we all be moved in our hearts to feel your pain and then have that pain flow through our hands in service.

I see you. We see you!

In loving memory of
Jason King and Reverend Elroy Moore

CONTENTS

FOREWORD

Dave Gibbons

*They thought they buried us, but
they didn't know we were seeds.*

Mexican Proverb

There is a lot of knowledge and many inspirational talks about dealing with systemic poverty and homelessness. Few dive into the hard work of justice and stay there. And even fewer individuals love without any conditions.

Terence is one of those few. He walked 648 miles from his home to Washington, DC, to raise awareness of those who are fighting for their lives in the dark places of our cities and another four hundred miles to the Lorraine Motel in Memphis for the same cause on behalf of the MLK50 celebration. Terence was buried with life in ways that would have caused many of us to quit, but he got up and started walking.

We live in an insight-intoxicated culture where we believe change is about the insight that we heard and got chills from. It can be at a conference or in a church service or perhaps listening to a favorite inspirational podcast. While endorphins may be released and cause a physical sensation in us when we hear an insight, the truth is we haven't changed. The truth is we haven't done anything. We felt something but didn't act on the reality that was unveiled.

What I love about this book is how Terence shares from his own struggles. In fact, he goes beyond his own story of suffering and chooses to enter the space of others who are seeking something more. Instead of choosing the most naturally gentrified and hipster place to go, he goes to the places where beauty isn't immediately evident.

As a man on a mission, Terence passionately searches for seeds planted in a place that may be dark and dirty beneath the surface where most look. The context of the pain he writes from is real and strikes the heart. He's not seeking sympathy but provides hope for all of us who suffer too. Terence challenges us not to charity but to love without strings, without boundaries. As you read these pages you can see how this book is not simply talking about poverty or misconceptions around poverty, but Terence lays out real, proven ways to practically address poverty.

For the last fourteen years of his life, Terence has wholly dedicated his life, with the loving partnership of his wife and family, to serve those who are vulnerable and within the death grip of poverty. He saw firsthand while growing up the severe challenges and traumas associated with poverty. His soft-spoken voice and his gentleness emerge from these dark places.

Terence is wholly committed to his family and to his family of friends in the middle of a painful journey. Terence humbly and lovingly disrupts attitudes and beliefs about those suffering in poverty. He's highly creative, passionate, pragmatic, and sacrificial. This comes out in everything he does. You see his laser focus, resilience, and joy as he serves those who are often not seen, the misfits and the marginalized. He started a nonprofit, which is a natural extension of his heart, called Love Beyond Walls.

So devour this book and let Terence gently speak to you from his soul. He will help you see poverty differently. He won't let you stay in despair but will lead you to the promised land of hope where real solutions and love await. Get ready for deep reflections that will lead you to love beyond walls and to be the change. Let's go with Terence to the places where others dare not go. Let's break through the darkness and discover more seeds ready to see the light of day.

Walking with you, Terence!

INTRODUCTION

SEARCHING FOR HOME

One Friday morning in November, I went to visit my friend Kurt, who happened to be homeless at the time, and take him breakfast. I pulled up to an abandoned building in downtown Atlanta where I could usually find him. I saw him on the other side of the rusty fence that surrounded the building. He crawled through a small slit in the barrier, and we stood in front of my car to talk. Trash covered the ground where Kurt and others had made a place to stay.

I turned to Kurt and asked, "Hey, would you mind if I took your picture?"

"Yeah, man," he said, "what do you want to use it for?"

I responded, "You know, I would just like to tell your story. To tell people about the realities of what you have to go through."

"I'll make you a deal," he said. "If you get me a pillow, I'll let you take my picture."

"Okay. Why don't you go get the pillow you have now?" I suggested. "You can hold it up over your face so no one will see you. I'll take this picture and post it on social media to tell people my friend needs a pillow. We'll see who wants to step up and notice you." (It didn't take more than an hour for someone to commit to buying him a pillow.)

We talked a while longer. We laughed, joked about life and fast food. Kurt and I had been friends for a little over three months at this point, and I felt like we were close enough to ask him about his plans.

I said to him, "Hey man, it's cold. It's only going to get colder."

Even as I spoke, I could see white vapor leaving my mouth.

I continued, "Let me take you to a shelter . . ." He cut me off almost immediately.

"No, no, no, no. I'm not doing a shelter."

"Why? At least there you'll be out of the elements."

He described the shelter he had been to nearby—the smell and the number of people in the rooms, how he had to sleep in chairs and that there was only one bathroom. And the crime there made it impossible to sleep anyways.

"It's more comfortable here," he said as he pointed at the trash in the waste field we were standing in. "It's more comfortable here than in one of those shelters."

Then he said, "I bet you won't sleep in the shelter. I bet you couldn't last a night in there. And if you did, I bet you'd be right here on the backside of this building with me before the night's up."

I was shocked. His challenge popped my comfort bubble.

"I'll do it. I'll go sleep in that shelter!" I told him. At the time, I don't think either of us really thought I would do it.

He laughed, "Yeah, man? I don't believe you. You're gonna have to show me."

We continued joking and spent another hour or two talking before I told him I had to go and get his pillow.

I got in my car with the idea swirling in my mind. Three weeks later, I came back to visit my friend Kurt and told him I was going to stay in the shelter. However, the shelter idea didn't happen the way I planned. Instead, I ended up living under a bridge in the heart of Atlanta with about fifty other people living in tents.

From the comfort of our own homes it's hard to understand the complexities of something like poverty and homelessness. It requires listening to the stories of those who experience it: the children born into homelessness, people who end up destitute because of a loss of a loved one or unexpected health challenges, youth on the streets due to instability in their families or because they identify with the LGBTQ+ community, women trying to escape domestic abuse, and people who lost a job of significant income. Whether or not you've ever experienced this type of homelessness and poverty, there are universal principles we relate to when it comes to searching for a home.

MY SEARCH FOR HOME

For a long time, I wasn't sure why I was so drawn to helping those experiencing poverty and homelessness. While it was something I had grown up around, I had never lived on the streets for an extended period of time. As I wrote this book, though, I began to realize why I felt this way and why you might too.

My parents split up when I was a young, and growing up I watched my mom struggle as a single mother. She did everything in her power to ensure my little sister and I didn't have to worry about where we would stay or what we would eat. In fact, Mom was my first hero and showed me at an early age the power of hard work and resilience. However, my parents' split confused me, and in many ways it haunts me to this day. I'm not sure if a child fully recovers from splits, but I know they never forget. Looking back, this event led me to start looking for a home. It caused me to question what made a home a home and why mine seemed to vanish so suddenly.

I internalized many of the things I went through as a child, and it landed me in a lot of trouble during my teen years. I was a living statistic: a not-so-good relationship with my father, at risk, and making poor decisions. I'll never forget the day I rebelled so strongly against my mom that I left home and lived out of the trunk of my car. I was a mid-teen, misguided, and searching for my identity. I told Mom I wanted to drop out of high school, a common narrative for a young African American man without a father present in the home. She told me if I wanted to live at her house I had to go to school, so I moved out. Looking back, I guess I ran away.

Soon after I moved out I realized that education was one of the only ways out of the situation I was in, so I reenrolled in classes but continued to live in my car at the park near my school or in different friends' homes. Mom often did not know where I was. I can only imagine the type of stress I inflicted on her. One friend, Jeremy, who was eighteen and was working at the time, found out I was living in my car and asked his mom if I could stay with them for a few days. It was his mom's yes that helped me get through school and keep going when I felt like giving up. The few days ended up turning into almost a full school year.

Jeremy spent his nights working. When he came home in the morning, he would tell me to go to school. He gave me money to buy lunch at school so I wouldn't go hungry. Some days his encouragement and support was the only reason I kept going to school. I got dressed out of clothes in a garbage bag that I'd grabbed from my mom's house and attempted to go to school with a clear mind. It was beyond hard because I was going to school with borrowed strength from a few friends and Jeremy's mom—and anybody else who thought I could do it.

Moving around as a teen, feeling deeply misunderstood, and not understanding the dysfunction stemming from my family were the manifestations of what was happening internally. I was looking for a safe, stable place to belong. The search for a home was a different kind of longing than the pursuit of four walls with a white picket fence. It's a search that began in my childhood, stayed with me throughout my teens, and followed me into adulthood. Where do I belong? is a question I've been asking deep in my bones.

Have you ever asked that question?

Where do we belong? Where is our home? What is *home*?

WHAT IS HOME?

Home is more than four walls and a roof. It's more than the place where you put your head down at night or where you store your most valuable possessions.

Home is where you feel safe—a place with people you can count on and where you can be yourself. Home is a place of unconditional belonging. No matter what you do or where you go, home is the place you can come back to and belong. It might not even be a place at all.

For some, home is a person or a group of people. Some people feel at home when they are in a small group at church or worshiping with their church family. Some people find home in places like barbershops or in beauty salons—among peers with whom they can discuss all of life's ills and social problems. Some people find home in book clubs and other environments where they connect with people who accept them fully and completely.

In his book *The Search to Belong*, Joseph R. Myers observes that everyone is looking for a front porch. He uses the analogy of the porch to symbolize a place of comfort, community, and acceptance.[1] Everyone is looking for a safe place that feels like home.

For many of us, though, the feeling of home and belonging is foreign. We might be more accustomed to feeling alone in a crowd or not being sure who to call in the middle of hardship. Maybe the people we were supposed to rely on weren't able to be there for us. Or maybe we've just never felt like we fully belonged.

Historically, the church has offered an invitation to those who don't have a home or a place of belonging. Jesus aims to bridge the gap and create a community of disconnected people looking for more than just a physical space to exist in. Jesus proclaims the good news that those who have been outsiders are accepted into the family of God and have a spiritual home that can never be tampered with or taken away. There's no greater freedom to someone who is oppressed and overlooked than words of welcome and acceptance. Jesus himself says,

> The Spirit of the Lord is on me,
>   because he has anointed me
>   to proclaim good news to the poor.
> He has sent me to proclaim freedom for the prisoners
>   and recovery of sight for the blind,
> to set the oppressed free,
>   to proclaim the year of the Lord's favor. (Luke 4:18-19)

This search for a place to belong is linked to what I call spiritual poverty. Deeper than the physical poverty you see when you look at a man pushing a shopping cart, spiritual poverty can be found in both you and me. This hunger comes not from a lack of food but a lack of connection, belonging, acceptance, and being in relationship with God. Instead of searching for a shelter, the spiritually poor look for a place to belong and to be loved.

Recognizing our own spiritual poverty helps us understand where the concept of poverty comes from. When we are able to listen to someone else's story with an open heart and hear their experience, which may look different than ours, we begin to close the gap between them and us. Having an open mind means learning to add more to our already-existing beliefs about affirming the dignity of those who are impoverished.

Altogether, if we are committed to doing this heart-and-mind work, we may encounter new people or ideas. We might not agree with them all, but that is how we begin to see and love people as Jesus did.

WHAT IS POVERTY?

The reality of poverty and homelessness is difficult to grasp. It's wrapped up in politics, economics, systems, formulas for solutions, and a hundred other seemingly complicated barriers. On one hand, systemic poverty *is* complicated. There are hundreds of contributing factors. On the other hand, poverty can be simple.

According to the government, poverty includes any family of four making less than $28,290 a year. But it doesn't include that same family if they make $28,291. While we assign a particular number to what qualifies as "poverty," we miss the greater humanity and complexity tied to these situations. I propose we redefine poverty. Poverty is a *lack of access*.

People experience different levels of poverty when they lack access to good education, clean water, job opportunities, resources, health care, healthy food, and other basic needs, including money, but not limited to that. In *Jesus and the Disinherited* Howard Thurman gives some definition to those who have their backs against the wall in society and culture. He identified those persons as the poor, the disinherited, and the dispossessed. He writes,

> I can count on the fingers of one hand the number of times that I have heard a sermon on the meaning of religion, of Christianity, to the man who stands with his back against the wall. It is urgent that my meaning be crystal clear. The masses of men live with their backs constantly against the wall. They are the poor, the disinherited, the dispossessed. What does our religion say to them? The issue is not what it counsels them to do for others whose need may be greater, but what religion offers to meet their own needs. The search for an answer to this question is perhaps the most important religious quest of modern life.[2]

It's true that impoverished people have their backs against the wall. But a greater truth is that this kind of poverty does not exclude people from finding home in the family of God.

Over the last fifteen years of working closely with those experiencing poverty and homelessness, I've found that one of the greatest hindrances to helping them overcome their circumstances is how others perceive them.

Most common assumptions about the poor are:

- They are lazy and uneducated.
- They chose to be poor. They could pick themselves up by their bootstraps and get out of it if they *really* wanted to.
- The poor are the government's responsibility.
- I can't understand or relate to the poor.
- The poor are criminals.
- It's their own fault they're poor.

- I don't know how to help them.
- There's nothing we can do. There will always be homeless and poor people.
- They have great spiritual and moral issues.

In *The Rich and the Rest of Us*, Cornel West and Tavis Smiley quote Barbara Ehrenreich to help us to see how negative misconceptions of the poor have always been a factor in why the poor are mistreated and demonized. Ehrenreich says, "The theory for a long time—coming not only from the right but also from some Democrats—is that poverty means that there's something wrong with your character, that you've got bad habits, you've got a bad lifestyle, you've made the wrong choices."[3]

In this book I want to help deconstruct some of the misconceptions we have about the poor and tell you the stories of those who are experiencing poverty. Take a moment and ask yourself, *How do I see the poor? What do I believe to be true of those experiencing homelessness and poverty?* And maybe even more importantly, evaluate where those beliefs came from.

Sometimes our beliefs are passed down from a parent, from the news media, or from our peers. But our preconceived notions about the poor are rarely true. What if all those assumptions weren't true? We can never fully know a person until we get close to them. In 1962 at Cornell College in Mount Vernon, Iowa, Martin Luther King Jr. explained,

> I am convinced that men hate each other because they fear each other. They fear each other because they don't know each other, and they don't know each other because they don't communicate with each other, and they don't communicate with each other because they are separated from each other.[4]

His words ring true today. To really understand something, we often need to experience it for ourselves or at least hear the story of someone who has experienced it. So, as you've formed beliefs and ideas about the poor and homeless, have you ever experienced homelessness or spoken to someone who has? Do you fear people who are experiencing this plight because you have been separated from them?

In the rest of this book you're going to hear those stories, as well as my own story, of experiencing homelessness. To take this journey I'm not asking you to abandon your home physically, but you must at least be willing to mentally engage in the exploration. If you do, this book will bring you on a journey of understanding the poor differently. We'll talk through stereotypes, misconceptions, responsibilities, and solutions to the poverty epidemic. You might also learn something about your own poverty along the way.

First, you must ask yourself if you're willing to examine the way you think and the things you believe about the poor. Having an open mind may mean listening to someone else who comes from a walk of life different from yours. Having an open mind may mean listening to a perspective that doesn't necessarily align with your set of beliefs. I've learned that it is extremely hard to dislike or hate someone up close. When you get to know a person's hopes, fears, dreams, and thoughts about the future, you see how much you have in common. If you want to honor God, get to know someone unlike you.

When a thread starts to unravel in a piece of clothing, the entire garment is threatened because the thread does not stand alone. The thread, although apparently isolated, is connected to the entire fabric. The owner of the piece of clothing would be foolish to say, "Allow the thread to suffer because it caused its own hardship." No, the owner would say, "Let me care for the thread because it hurts that entire piece of clothing."

What if we had this same approach to caring for the poor, if we chose to see one person's suffering as being a part of the much larger fabric of humanity? Together we wrestle to find dignity, worth, and security. Through the long search, many of us find answers through faith that rescues us from the poverty that plagued our souls long before our economic status was defined. Let's start seeing people.

CHAPTER ONE

DEMYSTIFYING POVERTY

Have you ever felt like a fraud? That at any moment the people around you might find you out and realize that you weren't as good as they thought you were? In 2013 I found myself wondering this while I prepared to live on the streets for a week. I was doing this, in part, because I promised my friend Kurt that I would stay in a shelter one night to try to convince him that the shelter was better than the street. (I was wrong about that.) I also decided on this experiment because I knew that I needed to understand homelessness firsthand, even if only for a week. While there's a huge difference between living on the streets by choice and because there are no other options, I had to get as close to it as possible.

The night before I was to live among those experiencing homelessness, I didn't sleep at all. I wondered how I would get food, a tent, or how I would survive the below-freezing temperatures at night and the rain that was expected in downtown Atlanta for the next week. I thought about my safety and what my kids would think of me as they watched me do this. I doubted whether the idea would make any impact or matter at all. I wrestled with questions:

What's going to change if I do this?
Would I be able to help anyone?
Am I the right person to do this?

The fears, doubts, and questions swirled in my mind until the morning came. I had already told a lot of people that I was going to do it, so I couldn't back out now. (But I did think about it.)

That night, my wife and kids drove me to the spot where I was going to sleep. We pulled up under the bridge on the side of the interstate.

Cecilia turned to me. "It's time," she said. "There's no turning back."

My daughter, Zion, in the back seat asked, "Dad are you going to help some people?"

"I hope so," I told her.

I opened the door to the back seat of the car and hugged my three-year-old son and six-year-old daughter, "I'll be home on Christmas. I love you."

The sun had already set and I could barely see the tents of the other people who called the space under the bridge their home. The ground was damp from the rain that made its way from the hill next to us.

I walked up to the group of people huddled around one another. I had visited a few days before and told them I was coming. A man named Robert, one of the guys who stayed in this area, recognized me from before and ran over to me with open arms.

He had lived on the streets on and off since his early teens. He came from a single mom who struggled with drug abuse, and not long after he followed in her footsteps, leading him to his current situation. Robert made me think about the many people searching for a place to call home.

Robert was one of the friendliest guys you'd ever meet— humble, funny, welcoming. He was the first person to talk to me and ask me my story.

Immediately after learning why I was there, Robert took it upon himself to collect a bunch of things that I was going to need to survive. He walked around to the different tents and groups of people curled up in blankets to see if anyone had extras. To my surprise, it didn't take long for him to round up a tent and a few blankets from their already limited resources. I tried to tell him I couldn't take those supplies, that they needed them more than me, but he insisted. "We have to stick together," he told me, "this is how it works here." His reassuring words and the wind blowing through my sweatshirt wore my resistance down, and I thanked him and the others for their kind welcome.

I set up my tent and my blankets, and it almost looked as if I were merely on a camping trip, but as I looked around me, the sick, the hungry, the cold, and the hopeless definitely were not on a camping trip. These people were fighting for their lives.

Another man walked over to my tent, and Robert introduced us. Mark also was living under the bridge, so I asked him how long he had lived here. As we were talking, others in the group decided to walk to a shelter to charge their phones and try to get food. We decided to join them. It was still pouring and windy, but we continued walking through the elements for what I shortly found out was a mile and a half walk.

We finally made it to the shelter, soaked through and shivering from the freezing cold. The shelter downtown was crowded; the only spots for us to sit were on the ground or on a few metal chairs scattered throughout the lobby area. Just as we were starting to warm up and revive our dead phones, an employee told us, "Hey, you guys gotta get going. We're closing for the night."

I looked around at my friends and thought about having to go back outside in the elements. I asked the worker, "Do you think we could just stay here for a while? It's cold outside, about to drop to ten degrees tonight."

He said, "Don't get mad at me because you chose this life" (his exact words).

Unsure how to respond, my friends and I gathered our stuff and made our way back outside. Tasha leaned over and said to me, "See, this is how they treat you when you're homeless." I kept asking myself, *How do you find home when you are being treated like this?*

I later learned that this particular shelter stopped allowing people to sleep overnight in the lobby, and people experiencing homelessness could only stay there for short periods of time before they had to move on to another place. However, the shelter did have programs on different floors where those experiencing homelessness could sleep. To sleep there, however, a person had to be addicted to a substance, and each program only could take a certain amount of people.

"Come on. There's another shelter a mile down the road," Mark said. I couldn't imagine walking another mile in the rain and cold, but I quietly followed. We still hadn't had anything to eat for dinner, so I asked Mark how we were going to get food. "I don't know," he said. "Pray. Pray someone will bring us something."

No one brought us anything, though, and the next shelter didn't have anything to offer or any space. We were turned away, still wet, still cold. Mark said our best bet was to beg for food. He brought me to a busy street corner where we stood in the rain begging for money to get something to eat. My cell phone was dying, my socks and shoes were wet, and no one gave us anything. With no other options or places to go, we decided to go home. We walked back to our spots under the bridge, and I crawled into my tent and thought that maybe if I slept the night would go by faster.

I didn't have any cardboard or anything to put under the tent. So when I laid down on the thin, vinyl tent bottom, I felt every rock, uneven surface, sharp edge, and the wet dirt of the ground beneath me.

I only lasted a few minutes before I got out of my tent to ask Robert, "How do you do that? Just sleep on the ground like that?"

"I don't know, you just sleep through it."

Back in my tent, I laid down on the rocks and tried to fall asleep. My toes were numb in the wet December cold. The gravel seemed harder from the temperature drop. Some tents were close together because the closeness added a little extra heat—or maybe not. People were frustrated with the weather and wondering if they would make it through the night. I wondered the same thing.

After a few minutes, I heard people next to my tent cursing at each other. A woman was yelling at the man beside her, "Where is it? Where is it?" The man responded over and over again, "I don't know. I don't know what you're talking about."

I slipped my head outside my tent to see what they were fighting about. They told me they were missing a case of water. I rolled over in my tent and listened to them fight for a few more minutes. I wasn't used to people fighting about a basic need. No one was cutting someone's car off in traffic or arguing about where to get dinner. They were fighting about water!

The cycle of trying to sleep, getting up, talking to the others outside, losing feeling in my fingers and toes, and then trying to sleep again went on all night. That's when I started talking with a guy named Sam. We stood outside by a bin where the community was burning extra clothes that had been donated to keep warm through the night. Sam was quiet but eventually told me a little about himself. He told me he married young but found out his wife had cheated on him. She also gave him HIV and shortly after that left him.

He moved to Atlanta and got a temp job but continued to wrestle with depression and isolation. Eventually, his depression consumed him; he couldn't get up to go to work and didn't know what to do to address his depression. His uncertainty about how to deal with everything drew him deeper into physical poverty, which landed him on the side of the interstate with dozens of others. It saddens me every time I think about his isolation.

I asked him about my feet: "Man, what do you do? My toes are cold." That's when he went into his tent and brought me out his last pair of donated socks.

"You don't need these?" I queried.

"Nah, man, you can use them. You gotta get through the night."

Completely surprised and astonished by the generosity of these people who had so little, I told him I couldn't take his socks, that he needed them more. Together, we stared at the fire for a few more minutes. I saw my friend Mark on one of the hills that overlooked the highway next to the baseball stadium. I walked next to him and stood by him for a few minutes in silence. We watched the cars pass by us.

Mark broke the silence, "See, bro, this is why I respect you. 'Cause most churches, they come out here, pass out stuff, and they leave. We may never see them again, but you stay with us."

He continued, "Look at the cars. Look at all these people just passing by. Why don't people stop and see us? They know we up here. They know we up here."

He shook his head and repeated, "They know we up here . . . they know we up here."

And he was right. We do know. We know that millions of people go to bed hungry in our country. Thousands of these people are in our cities. Many of them are in our neighborhoods and right next door.

What separates us? What keeps us at arm's length? What creates this mystifying divide?

THE TRUTH OF OVERCOMING POVERTY

If we're honest, at best we're apathetic toward the poor and the men, women, and children who live under the bridges. Most of us have actually been taught to act this way. What did your parents do when you drove past someone begging on the street? Look straight ahead. Don't make eye contact. I bet we do something similar with the poor, the homeless. Most of us ignore these people.

A few months ago I was visiting New York City and rode the subway with a friend who lived there. A man begging for change got onto our car, and my friend leaned over and said, "Just don't look at him. If you acknowledge him, he won't leave you alone. Ignore him." I was surprised by his blunt instructions on how to avoid the struggling man in front of us, but I think he said what most people are thinking.

It's easier to look past them even when they stand next to our windows in the dark and pouring rain. We rationalize it too: "What could I really do anyway? What if they spend the money on alcohol? And I don't have any cash." So it's easier to stare ahead and choose not to see people faced with extreme hardship. Why? Because the moment we choose to acknowledge someone in pain, we have to decide whether we will respond with love, generosity, and grace.

I'm willing to bet most of you reading this feel an awkward tug or feel like you should do more. But when the light turns green we quickly forget that the man on the curb is still standing hungry in the rain.

In the United States, we live within systems with policies that help some people and hurt others. Today, many would say that the United States is as fair and equitable as it ever has been. I think that sentiment has some truth in it, but there are some things we need to remember that help us make sense of the present we now live in.

The civil rights movement ended in 1968. Just fifty years ago, African American men, women, and children were fighting to be seen as equal under the US law. Only *fifty* years ago people were denied basic civil rights because of their skin color. A huge part of our population today lived through that movement. How, then, can we rationally believe that the effects are no longer felt of a system and government that only fifty years ago oppressed an entire race? The effects, the bias, and the pain are still felt. In the same way that systemic racism still has lingering effects today, our society still feels the effects of a system that lifts others up while pushing others down. This has more factors than race, and we're going to explore specific causes behind poverty, but for now we're talking about a bigger picture.

There is a greater narrative, a larger one, where people are treated differently, and some people are treated like they are less than human because of the way they look, what they have, who they know, their socioeconomic status, and more. In Scripture God despises such disdain toward the poor and marginalized. In Proverbs, Solomon writes this powerful truth:

> Do not exploit the poor because they are poor
>   and do not crush the needy in court,

for the LORD will take up their case
and will exact life for life. (Proverbs 22:22-23)

We must begin to fight against the notion that we and the powers that control our society have authority to treat anyone unfairly and unequally. When we benefit from a system, it is difficult to see the injustice behind it, and it can be even harder to change in a way that might not benefit us. A well-known quote on the internet by author David Gaider echoes this sentiment: "Privilege is when you think that something's not a problem because it's not a problem for you personally."[1]

For a while I struggled with the idea of how to help people get out of poverty and homelessness. When I was young, I bought into the American motto "Anyone can achieve the American dream" and that if you were struggling you just needed to "pull yourself up by your bootstraps and work harder!" These beliefs are ingrained in our culture, so why would we care about people on the streets who should be able to work harder and pull themselves out of their situation?

Research from the Brookings Institution shows that it's actually much more likely for the rich to stay rich and the poor to stay poor.

> Stagnant incomes and falling wages have meant that fewer Americans are growing up to be better off than their parents. Upward absolute intergenerational mobility was once the almost-universal experience among America's youth. No longer. Among those born in 1940, about 90 percent of children grew up to experience higher incomes than their parents, according to researchers at the Equality of Opportunity Project. This proportion was only 50 percent among those born in the 1980s.[2]

Johns Hopkins University researchers followed eight hundred students for twenty-five years and found that students' futures were mostly determined by the families they were born into.

> At nearly 30 years old, almost half the sample found themselves at the same socio-economic status as their parents. The poor stayed poor; those better off remained better off.
>
> Only 33 children moved from birth families in the low-income bracket to the high-income bracket as young adults; if family had no bearing on children's mobility prospects, almost 70 would be expected. And of those who started out well off, only 19 dropped to the low-income bracket, a fourth of the number expected. . . . Of the children from low-income families, only 4 percent had a college degree at age 28, compared to 45 percent of the children from higher-income backgrounds.[3]

There are dozens of reasons that this cycle of poverty continues. Let's look at and break down one of the simplest barriers to overcoming poverty. (Keep in mind this is only a small picture of a complex problem.) One of the first steps to getting out of poverty, or at least off of the streets, is to get a job. At its most basic, people experiencing poverty need resources and money to get the things they need to survive. For example, let's use a well-abled person—not someone who is elderly, a disabled veteran, or suffering from chronic illness, all presenting even more challenging barriers to overcome—someone you and I see on the street who could, theoretically, get a job.

Logistically, when you get a job, unless you're mowing your neighbor's lawn or doing other odd jobs, you'll need an ID. In my home state of Georgia, here are the different things you'll need to apply for an ID:

- Proof of your identity, like a passport or birth certificate, and proof of your Social Security number (one document), like your Social Security card (original or copy), or a W-2 form. (Most adults in general don't know where their birth certificate or social security card is, especially people living on the streets or in and out of temporary housing. If you're looking to get an ID to get a job, you probably won't have access to a W-2 form either.)

- Proof of your Georgia residency (two documents), such as a utility bill issued within the last two years, a financial statement issued within the last two years (bank, credit card, etc.), or a current rental agreement. Again, this provides challenges for people transitioning out of homelessness or who struggle with housing—to prove that they live in one place or have a bank account.

- Payment for your ID card fee—$32. This is also an interesting barrier. For most of us, this amount of money probably doesn't feel like much, and it probably doesn't seem like a big deal. But imagine that you are someone trying to prove your identity, to prove that you exist, and because you can't come up with an extra $32, you are denied. You cannot prove your identity without even a (small) monetary amount.

An article in the *Washington Post* quotes lawyer Chad W. Dunn:

I hear from people nearly weekly who can't get an ID either because of poverty, transportation issues or because of the government's incompetence. Sometimes government officials don't know what the law requires. People take a day off work to go down to get the so-called free birth certificates.

People who are poor, with no car and no Internet access, get
up, take the bus, transfer a couple of times, stand in line for
an hour and then are told they don't have the right documents or it will cost them money they don't have. A lot of
them just give up.[4]

These are just the obstacles to getting an ID card. That's is only
the first step to getting a job.

Let's say that someone beats these odds. They get an ID and
maybe even get a job that pays the 2018 minimum wage in
Georgia, $7.25 per hour. Working forty hours a week, they'll
make $290 each week, potentially $15,080 a year. Could you live
on that with your current responsibilities and lifestyle?

Most families living in poverty are single-income households.
That means that this yearly salary of $15,080 supports a family
of three or four people. This leads to terrible living conditions,
malnourished children, and people with little or no help to
escape poverty. With the cost of everything going up and wages
staying the same, this makes it hard for people to live stable lives.
Now add in the unexpected circumstances that come out of
nowhere—the death of a spouse, a speeding ticket, or having to
buy medication for an uncontrollable illness.

We're just talking numbers. We're not talking the quality of
life and the compounded emotional toll of growing up poor.
Arthur Dobrin reported a Boston Children's Hospital study that
concluded that severe psychological and physical neglect pro-
duces measurable changes in children's brains.[5]

Children living in poverty experience high levels of stress
because, while they're hungry and not sure where they're going
to sleep next week, they often live in violent neighborhoods,
move residences twice as often and get evicted five times more

than the average American, and are more likely to be bullied in school.

Stress and poverty are interdependent. Those living in these conditions are fighting for access to good health care and a way to embrace healthier lifestyles, and the chronic stress puts them at a higher risk for heart disease, high blood pressure, diabetes, and depression. Can you imagine trying to maintain a healthy, balanced lifestyle while fighting every possible thing that makes you more vulnerable? Escaping poverty's among the physical barriers is difficult, but with the added emotional toll, it's almost impossible. It's not as simple as we'd like to think. I was blown away when I read an *Atlantic* article by Gillian B. White titled "Escaping Poverty Requires Almost 20 Years with Nearly Nothing Going Wrong." She writes,

> A lot of factors have contributed to American inequality: slavery, economic policy, technological change, the power of lobbying, globalization, and so on. In their wake, what's left?
>
> That's the question at the heart of a new book, *The Vanishing Middle Class: Prejudice and Power in a Dual Economy*, by Peter Temin, an economist from MIT. Temin argues that, following decades of growing inequality, America is now left with what is more or less a two-class system: One small, predominantly white upper class that wields a disproportionate share of money, power, and political influence and a much larger, minority-heavy (but still mostly white) lower class that is all too frequently subject to the first group's whims.
>
> Temin identifies two types of workers in what he calls "the dual economy." The first are skilled, tech-savvy workers

and managers with college degrees and high salaries who are concentrated heavily in fields such as finance, technology, and electronics—hence his labeling it the "FTE sector." They make up about 20 percent of the roughly 320 million people who live in America. The other group is the low-skilled workers, which he simply calls the "low-wage sector."[6]

POVERTY AND DIGNITY

A friend of mine, John, works with kids who live in low-income housing in Atlanta. He grew close to one family in particular and started to assist the children's mom in getting back on her feet, especially in relation to getting assistance like food stamps.

They walked into the government building located far outside the city. It took about forty-five minutes to drive there, but to get to the building by public transit would take about three hours. John and Nancy walked into a small room that had ten computers set up on one side with fifty people waiting to use them. All of the computers had complicated login instructions next to them.

"For me, someone who uses computers and knows how to read," John told me, "the instructions were extremely complicated."

The instructions said to *not* fill out the form correctly. Fill out the first form incorrectly to gain access to the system. The computer system hadn't been updated, so anyone trying to renew had to instead say that they had never received food stamps before so they could access the application.

"After that, there's an application with a bunch of questions. It still took us an hour and a half to submit the form," John said.

Nancy wasn't able to read the instructions, so John sat with her and went through each question and helped her write out the answers.

"These are people who can't really read and people who haven't used computers much. I saw two people walk out and not even finish the application. There was only one woman there to help the ten people using the computers."

Even after the application is submitted, it's not approved right away, so you don't walk out with food stamps.

John then told me, "I asked the woman who was working if there was anything that could help my friend Nancy in the meantime. She had run out of food stamps and didn't have any food. I had heard of emergency food stamps and wanted to know if my friend was eligible. The woman looked back at me and kind of snapped, 'You can buy her some food.' That was the only option presented for someone who didn't have any food.

"There was no dignity in this system," he concluded.

People cannot beat the system, nor is it helpful to the people trying to get out of poverty. I want to demystify the idea that poverty is always a choice, that there is a formula to follow to get out of poverty, and that poverty can be ignored by those it does not touch.

I often recognize that this very well could have been me in this situation. Some of us don't realize that in a moment, without a support system that can provide for us, our entire lives can be turned upside down.

A few months ago a woman in a white Mercedes pulled up to our nonprofit center on a day we were giving out groceries to families in need. A Mercedes doesn't often pull up to our center for resources, so heads turned in the direction of the expensive car. The woman got out of her car and stood in line.

I walked up to her and asked, "Hey, are you here to volunteer?"

"No," she responded, "I'm here because I hear you guys are giving out resources."

"Would you mind walking with me a little? There's another entrance over here." We started to walk toward the back of the building. I asked her some questions so I could better understand where she was coming from.

"I'm embarrassed to be here right now," she burst out crying, "I lost my job six months ago, and I'm starting to lose everything. I have a doctorate degree. I was so ashamed to pull up here to even ask for assistance with groceries."

I share this story not to put down the wonderful lady but to communicate that everyone needs to be seen and that we are all one circumstance away from being on the other side.

I took her to the back entrance and tried remove her feelings of shame about coming to the center. The organization was able to help provide her with some resources.

I walked her back to her car and she started crying, gave me a hug and said, "Thank you for being here."

I want to be clear. I'm not puffing up myself or our organization because we helped someone going through a struggle, neither am I saying we should all solve the world's ills through charity. I'm simply sharing this story to display the type of support that refuses to allow people to fall through the cracks of society and be forgotten forever. This type of support not only will help fill temporary gaps but also remind the person that they are seen and have a home.

Every story of poverty is different, unique, and surprising. People arrive in these situations in myriad ways. The types of poverty are also diverse: physical (lacking a home or clothing) and spiritual (lacking connection, purpose, family, or love).

I'll never forget how the sharp rocks felt under the thin tent floor while I tried to sleep when I intentionally lived homeless. I won't forget what it felt like to walk in the cold rain and the deep shame of begging for change. I still remember the faces of those who walked past and ignored me, pretending I wasn't even there.

So what does this mean for us? For those of us who ended up with support, homes to sleep in, and enough money to buy groceries, what role do we play in something so seemingly complex and systemic? We must first recognize our privilege and move toward creating a more equitable environment for everyone to live in.

I make note of our spiritual poverty because it is one of the strongest connections we have to those who suffer from having less. Paul says Jesus himself became poor so we might become rich: "You know the grace of our Lord Jesus Christ, that though he was rich, yet for your sake he became poor, so that you through his poverty might become rich" (2 Corinthians 8:9). He is referring to richness in relationship with God. Jesus became poor that we might overcome spiritual poverty.

We should have this same mentality when we encounter the poor. We have all experienced what it's like to be rejected, ignored, and missing something we desperately want and need. I challenge you to think about those experiences and imagine what it would be like to be raised poor and live in constant need. What would you believe about yourself and your abilities? What would you believe about the world around you if you constantly experienced stress, hunger, and shame?

We are accustomed to overcomplicating the issue and making it about politics, theories, and numbers, but we forget we are talking about living and breathing people who matter to God.

We mystify it so it is just above our reach, out of our grasp to change or make an impact.

The Bible's command is simple,

> Speak up for those who cannot speak for themselves,
>> for the rights of all who are destitute.
> Speak up and judge fairly;
>> defend the rights of the poor and needy. (Proverbs 31:8-9)

Let's deconstruct our narratives of the poor and begin to address their needs and the injustices they face, and let's discuss how we can support an equitable community for everyone.

CHAPTER TWO

YOU DON'T HAVE TO FEAR

I want to do something," the woman said to me, "but I'm just . . . I'm just so afraid."

These moments are particularly difficult for me. They happen often enough though. Somewhere along the line, the people struggling with poverty and homelessness went from being the most vulnerable and marginalized to being viewed as villains to be feared.

Fear, by definition, is the feeling caused by the belief that someone or something is dangerous, likely to cause pain or pose a threat. We experience fear all the time. It's the suspense deep in your gut that grows as the roller coaster car inches its way slowly up the track. It's the adrenaline that rushes through your veins when someone jumps out of the dark and yells, "Boo!"

When did we start to associate these emotions with and feel them when looking at someone in need? And even more importantly, why?

The list of factors contributing to the fear is long. Race, politics, what our parents taught us, that one story we heard on the TV news, the movie we saw as a kid, all of these play a part in the fear. But I have found that this fear stems from a deeper place: what we do not know.

We fear the unknown.

We humans have always feared what and who we are unfamiliar with. We are more inclined to be in community with those who look and talk like us. There is a certain safety in the familiar. Have you ever traveled to a new city or place you had never been to before? It can feel uncomfortable and unsettling if you have to find your way around on your own. That's because it's uncharted, unknown territory.

For this same reason kids, and sometimes even adults, are afraid of the dark. If you cannot see, you cannot know, and the unknown can be terrifying. This is why we have turned those who are vulnerable and hungry into monsters.

The fear is a result of myths, biased news stories, misunderstood perceptions, political agendas, classism, and a culture that has taught us possessions create worth.

CULTURE, POSSESSIONS, AND WORTH

What would you believe to be true of me if I came to a meeting driving a Mercedes and wearing a suit and tie? You'd think, *Wow, he must be important.* Or, *What does he do?* How would your perceptions of me change if I showed up in an old, beaten up car and wearing stained clothes?

Culture has trained us to associate a person's physical possessions with their worth and status. Somehow we have collectively decided that having a bigger house, a nicer car, or the latest phone means that a person has more importance, more esteem, more value. And what happens when we assign worth to people based on their possessions? The way we begin to treat them and the people around them changes. We start to assign worth based on externals instead of on the internal worth and value God has assigned to every single person. The Scriptures clearly affirm that we are all created in God's image: "God created man in His *own* image; in the image of God He created him; male and female He created them" (Genesis 1:27 NKJV).

This image, or *imago Dei*, "refers most fundamentally to two things: first, God's own self-actualization through humankind; and second, God's care for humankind. To say that humans are in the image of God is to recognize the special qualities of human nature which allow God to be made manifest in humans."[1]

This means it doesn't matter what people own or possess or what part of town they reside in; everyone's worth should be grounded in the fact that they are created in the image of God. But when worth and value are measured solely on the basis of external things, it creates distance between those who have and those who don't. And we begin to separate ourselves based on a false sense of worth. Here's the reality: "In 2016, the U.S. was considered the most valuable beauty and personal care market in the world, generating approximately 84 billion U.S. dollars in revenue that year."[2] If we focus that much on outward appearance, how much more do we confuse worth?

Many of us would say we don't judge people based on their possessions. We try to rise above this, but it's taught to us at an early age. We are constantly bombarded by messages that make us feel like we are missing out if we don't have the best and newest technology and gadgets. We learn to misplace and misidentify worth.

I experienced this while I was living on the streets during my week living as a homeless person. One morning I woke up shivering on the cold ground. I wasn't sure how I had made it through the night and wasn't sure I could do it again, but the thought of the cold night was replaced with a new, more immediate concern: food. Outside my tent, I was met by some of my new friends, and we began discussing what we were going to do for breakfast.

One woman said, "We should all walk to McDonald's."

Knowing it was a two-and-a-half-mile walk, I asked if there was any place closer. I wasn't sure that my body would make it that far after two hours of sleeping on the hard, rocky ground.

She continued, "Sometimes you can stand there in front of the McDonald's and people will give you a dollar, and you can get something off the menu."

My stomach growled again and I decided it would be better to try walking with my friends than staying cold and hungry under this bridge.

We started our trek, and I led the pack. I was talking to one of the guys next to me when I noticed a group of men and women in suits on the sidewalk in front of us. One of the women tapped the man next to her on the shoulder, gestured toward us, and motioned to move to the other side of the street.

In disbelief, I watched them cross the street. I hadn't even been out on the streets a full week, but with one glance this group had already perceived my friends and me as dangerous, to be avoided, or better yet not having enough worth to be seen.

We continued to McDonald's. We sat down in a booth inside the restaurant and a family sat near us. I watched them too as they looked at my friends and me and then got up and moved to a table farther away.

It's difficult to explain what it's like to be feared because of your physical appearance, the color of your skin (for me there's an added complexity, being a black man in America), or even your lack of resources. It was as if my worth had suddenly disappeared; because I was homeless there was something fundamentally wrong with me. I was left wondering what we had done and why our presence on the sidewalk and in the booth made these people so uncomfortable. It feels terrible to be looked down on, to be seen as less, to be feared. I felt voiceless and unwanted. Perhaps that's why Mother Teresa said, "Being unwanted, unloved, uncared for, forgotten by everybody, I think that is a much greater hunger, a much greater poverty than the person who has nothing to eat."[3]

Our fear causes us to respond like this. We cross the street. We ignore the man on the corner. We look past the woman on the sidewalk pushing a shopping cart. We think that maybe if we pretend we can't see them, we're not responsible, or if we ignore them, they will go away. These moments when we choose to ignore the hurting and vulnerable right in front of us are some of the most damaging moments in these people's lives.

Classism, racism, and prejudice have seeped into our beliefs, even unconsciously, causing us to respond with fear and create a greater distance between us and those who are poor. While we are pursuing more money, bigger houses, and more comfortable lifestyles, the lens through which we see the poor shifts from empathy to apathy. We start associating worth and value based on possessions and not on the inner worth and value God has given each person.

How we see other people can reveal where we are in our journey of addressing our own inner spiritual poverty. If our view of the poor is critical or apathetic, it may mean that we have not been filled with the wealth of God's love. Jesus said that we are to love God with everything and love our neighbor as ourselves. Our love toward our neighbors should be an outpouring of the love we have experienced from God.

The apostle John wrote,

> We love because he first loved us. Those who say, "I love
> God," and hate their brothers or sisters, are liars; for
> those who do not love a brother or sister whom they
> have seen, cannot love God whom they have not seen.
> The commandment we have from him is this: those who
> love God must love their brothers and sisters also.
> (1 John 4:19-21 NRSV)

The verse is straightforward; it's hard to say you love the unseen God when you don't love people right in front of you.

To walk past and ignore people is the same as saying, "You don't matter. You are not important." We are showing them with our actions that they are not valuable enough for us to stop and see and hear their pain. As a person of faith, I believe that love should compel us know those who lack love.

I wonder if those businessmen and businesswomen would have crossed the street if they knew me, if they knew my story or had seen a picture of my wife and kids. What would it have taken for me to prove to these people that they didn't need to fear me? More importantly, why was their first reaction fear?

How did fear become the starting point when people look at other human beings who simply have fewer possessions?

EVERYONE EQUAL?

One of the opening lines of the Declaration of Independence states, "We hold these truths to be self-evident, that all men are created equal, that they are endowed by their Creator with certain unalienable Rights, that among these are Life, Liberty and the pursuit of Happiness."

As a person of faith, I believe that our worth is based on the idea that all men and women are created equal because they are made in God's image. No person is born more valuable than another, regardless of their country of origin, the color of their skin, the social class they are born into, or the family they have. A person's value is not rooted in the furniture in their house, the clothes in their closet, the food in their pantry, or the lack thereof.[4]

Focusing on "*objective* social class entails a direct determination of a person's social class based on socioeconomic variables—mainly income, wealth, education and occupation. A second approach to social class, the one that occupies us here, deals with how people put themselves into categories."[5] Sociologists say there are generally five social classes. You've probably heard of them: upper class, upper-middle class, lower-middle class, working class, and poor. The classes are usually based on wealth, educational attainment, occupation, income, and membership in a subculture or social network.

In India, the caste system was a class structure determined by birth. A person born poor and in a lower caste would stay poor and in a lower caste. The same was true for someone born in an upper caste. There was no social mobility. India's caste system was abolished in 1949, but the effects of the system are still felt. The BBC explains its complexities:

> India's caste system is among the world's oldest forms of surviving social stratification. . . . The system which divides Hindus into rigid hierarchical groups based on their karma (work) and dharma (the Hindi word for religion, but here it means duty) is generally accepted to be more than 3,000 years old. . . . For centuries, caste dictated almost every aspect of Hindu religious and social life, with each group occupying a specific place in this complex hierarchy.[6]

The United States has no formal caste system that determines what job people will have and how much money they will earn. Instead, we have a capitalist system, "an economic system in which individual people make most of the decisions and own most of the property in a country."[7] In this system, there are free markets and competition for business and wealth. It means that things like the prison system and health care allow private parties to make money from what many consider to be fundamental rights.[8] This system can make it difficult for people in the working class and poor class to have equal opportunities. This happens when groups that have tremendous amounts of social and material access deny that same access to others who are in need.

So while we do not outwardly label people based on a caste they inherited by birth, many people are still not able to access things like health care, employment opportunities, healthy food, social capital, and good education because of the environment they were born into.

We inherit the socioeconomic status that our parents occupy, and most likely it's the same class that has been passed down through the generations. There is an idea in our culture that "anyone, regardless of his or her socioeconomic history or social position, can make it to the 'top' if he or she works hard."[9] That belief holds together the fabric the United States is built on. We would like to believe it is true. Unfortunately, that isn't exactly how it works.

The false narrative of the American dream was founded on the ideas of Horatio Alger.

Horatio Alger was a writer in American society, best known for his many writings that catered to a younger audience about impoverished boys and their rise from humble backgrounds to lives of middle-class security and comfort through hard work, determination, courage, and honesty. His writings were characterized by the "rags-to-riches" narrative, which had a formative effect on the United States during the Gilded Age.[10]

His narratives became popular in American culture, and Americans began to adopt the false ideas that people who were poor could work themselves out of oppression and impoverishment. However, we all know this is not true.

Initially, we placed people in classes based on gender, race, and age, and deemed some persons more worthy than others because of those characteristics. Today, we've come a long way and can't deny the progress we have made as a nation. But we still discriminate based on the numbers in a bank account, land owned, and the label on someone's jacket.

The Declaration of Independence states that "all men are created equal"; nevertheless, classism defines how each person is treated. Most public schools are funded by local property taxes. This means the richer the community, the more funding the school receives to educate students. Education is one of the leading forces in aiding people to earn a higher income. Children pay the price for living in a poorer district.

Individuals in the working class who work a full-time minimum-wage job still do not make enough money to pay their bills, feed their families, and save money to move or to invest in their futures. Currently in Georgia, minimum wage is $7.25.[11] Georgia still uses the federal minimum wage scale, and it's hard to make ends meet if you are making minimum wage. Some undoubtedly would say it's a start, and at least it's pay. But imagine how hard it would be to survive on such a low wage when inflation pushes prices up annually. How can the working poor get a job that pays more when they are working a job that matches the level of education they received?

I understand systemic poverty because I watched my mother struggle to feed us while working several jobs to climb the corporate ladder. My mother was fortunate to overcome and receive her doctoral degree in clinical counseling.

I understand discrimination because I've feared for my life because of the color of my skin. I know what it feels like to be told again and again that I am unworthy because of what I do or do not have. I've heard the stories of thousands of poor and homeless persons, and I've seen myself in all of them. I fought against the odds and wanted to give up.

I imagine you have felt this way too. The pain of the human experience binds us all in some way. We know what it is like to feel ashamed, not worthy, and forgotten. Poverty for many of us is tied to the number in our bank accounts, and for others it is tied to the messages we've heard all our lives. Either way, we are created equal because God created us. So how do we step out of a modern-day caste system and see one another as brothers and sisters in our journey through life?

A big reason we are so often tempted to associate someone's worth with their possessions or what they do is that we find our own worth in those things as well. The job we have, the neighborhood we live in, the car we drive, all contribute to the worth we believe we have.

Once we recognize that our own true worth is independent of our possessions, we can begin to see dignity and worth in those around us (and in ourselves).

Unfortunately, Jesus is portrayed as a white, middle-class man who was well liked. In *What Color Is Your God? Multicultural*

Education in the Church, James and Lillian Breckenridge stress the importance of having a gospel that is not monolithic but celebrates all ethnicities. They also reveal the pitfalls when we fail to do this.

In reality, though, Jesus associated with the poor and the marginalized, and was hated by most religious leaders. He brought good news that flipped traditional religious views. Why do we think it would be so different today? Do we believe that Jesus would belong to the same political party or church we subscribe to? Or would he tell us that caring for the poor and overlooked is our priority?

In his book *Jesus and the Disinherited*, Howard Thurman describes our current climate:

> Those people who live most obviously with their backs against the wall—for instance, the homeless, the working and jobless poor, the substance abused and abusers, the alienated, misguided, and essentially abandoned young people—are rarely within hearing or seeing range of the company of Jesus' proclaimed followers. The keepers of the faith of the master often find it very difficult, and very dangerous, to follow him into the hard places inhabited by the disinherited of America. And those wall-bruised people find no space for their presence in the places where the official followers are comfortably at worship.[12]

TO LIVE OUT OF FEAR

Fear can be a good thing. We listen to the fear that tells us to get out of the street when a car is heading toward us and when we get the feeling that maybe we shouldn't get close to the edge of a cliff. These fears are justified. Some fears keep us from good things too, even as they're trying to keep us safe. Have you ever feared a person you've begun to get close to? We fear to get too close to people who might hurt us or leave us, and we produce all sorts of defense mechanisms to protect ourselves. This fear can be less justified if we're only doing it out of past hurt.

There is a vast disparity though between living with the fears that keep us safe and letting our fears control us and the actions we take, especially when it comes to the way we treat other people—like crossing the street when we see someone dressed differently or building a wall to keep out those who might look or act different from us. Sometimes, doing nothing is a way we let our fears control us too.

What does it mean when the fear that paralyzes us has life-or-death implications for someone else? You're probably thinking, *No, no. My fear or inaction don't have that big of an impact on someone else's life.* Unfortunately, it does.

At its most basic level, fear keeps us from taking action. As fear evolves, though, it can often turn to apathy. We can grow cold and indifferent toward things we don't know or understand. This indifference toward the homeless and poor has dangerous implications. The apathy can come as a result of this resentment, privilege, and a lack of knowledge and concern for our brothers and sisters.

If we think the fear and demonization of the poor and homeless is to be taken lightly or that the implications are not important or urgent, here are some facts you need to know.

In 2014, violent fatal crimes against people experiencing homelessness increased by 61 percent over the previous year. That same year, nonlethal attacks also increased by 17 percent.[13] These attacks are becoming more common, and many experts attribute the attacks to the demonization of those experiencing homelessness.

In 2011, two men were charged with attacking a homeless man, videotaping the attack, and later posting the video online.[14] In 2012 a man in Los Angeles was charged with attempted murder after he set a homeless woman on fire as she slept on a bus bench where she had made her home for years.[15] There was no reported motive.

In 2014, the *Huffington Post* conducted an interview with Michael Stoops, then a director for the National Coalition for the Homeless, and reported, "The group found a direct correlation between the number of hate crimes exacted against homeless people and the criminalization of homelessness in those particular places."[16]

These statistics and surveys are more than just numbers to me. These vulnerable people are some of my friends, people who have changed my life.

Fear is dangerous. It creates an environment in which it's acceptable to treat those experiencing poverty and homelessness with anger and hate. The first step to stopping this is to realize that this fear is unfounded and dangerous.

Fear is sometimes rooted in ignorance, distance, and hatred. Hate in its basic form is a strong dislike toward persons or things, which is contrary to God. In the Bible, God hates only what dishonors both God and people. God hates hypocrisy and lies, wrongdoing, violence, idolatry, and things that aim to usurp God's righteousness and justice.

If fear of the poor and homeless has been a concern, you are fortunate poverty and homelessness have never been your reality. To live with fear like this is a sign of privilege. And if we are not careful, how we treat people because of our privilege can come off as hatred toward individuals who are harmless and powerless.

One day about a year ago, a woman pulled up to the Love Beyond Walls center and hopped out of the car with her two kids.[17] Her little girl was wearing an oversized T-shirt—no shoes, no underwear, just an adult T-shirt that was long enough to be a dress on her. The boy, slightly taller, wore a similar over-sized T-shirt but with shorts and oversized sneakers. Their hair was going in all different directions, and patches of dirt covered their faces as they stared down at the cement parking lot.

I turned to the woman and asked the same question I always ask someone I haven't seen before, "How did you hear about us?"

"I was at the gas station up the road," she said, "and the woman at the cash register told me about this place. I just drove here from Tennessee a couple weeks ago. I left to escape an abusive relationship. My kids and I have nowhere to go. We've just been staying in the car. The kids haven't been able to start school yet or anything. They need underwear and uniforms to start."

We brought the woman and her kids into the center and were able to provide them with uniforms and supplies. The words of this woman rang in my head. I'll never forget them: "I chose this. I chose this," she kept saying. "At least this is freer than being beat on."

Are these the people we fear? No, of course not. But that is only because her story is known. Every person experiencing poverty has a story, and many are similar to this one. I love what Rev. William Barber, the leader of the Poor People's Campaign, says when he is talking about honoring the stories of the poor: "Poverty is one of the great moral issues of our time." He is saying that we have got to stop stories like these from happening.

What happens when we remain silent or maintain the idea that those experiencing poverty are to be feared? I would be forced to look into this mother's eyes and tell her I can't help her due to government cuts in funding because fear creates a society that cares less and less about the hungry and vulnerable. I would be forced tell her that her choice to pursue freedom from domestic violence was in vain because the shelters are shutting down and there is nowhere for her to go as she makes this brave transition out of abuse. She's so desperate for change that she's been living out of her car for weeks.

We must stop spreading the idea that people are to be feared. We have to stop speaking of them as monsters and a drain on society. These perceptions are formed before we know their names or stories. Instead, we must begin to treat them with dignity. They want to be seen, to be heard, and to be given opportunities. Aren't we are all looking to put food on the table and keep our families safe and happy?

When we continue to approach others with fear, something in them begins to change. They grow accustomed to isolation. They begin to think, *Maybe I should be feared*, or *What if I am a monster?* One of the most damaging things I have seen is when someone experiencing poverty assumes it as their own identity, with no hope of getting out. This is what we should fear: that we provoke people into hopelessness with our untrue perceptions.

We treat people experiencing homelessness and poverty as if that is who they are. These people are not what they are experiencing. They are children, mothers, fathers, sisters, and brothers. Just because they wear their hardship outwardly does not give us the right to treat them as if their difficulty is their identity. It isn't. We have to start seeing people as going *through* problems instead of seeing people *as* problems.

Be someone who sees more than what culture and society train you to see in people facing these circumstances. Believe better in them so that they can believe better in themselves in return.

WHAT ABOUT CRIME?

It's true, the news reports ever-increasing crime statistics and stories of how dangerous it is on our city streets. The stats reveal that underresourced areas have a higher crime rate. And this fact alone creates fear in some. This is the very reason we need to be on the streets serving and helping these people, not just helping with basic needs but offering ourselves in the form of relationships to fill the social gaps in their lives. Crime is only a side effect of the real problem. The problem is a lack of resources and, in many instances, social capital.

So when we ask about the higher crime rates, we must also ask, do these people have access to food and meaningful relationships? It's true that there are higher crime rates in impoverished areas, but we must ask why. Is there an opportunity for the people in this community to thrive? Most often the answer is no, and then our initial question of why needs to be unraveled.

If you and your children are hungry, and you lost your job and have no way to feed them, what would you do? What if you have no one to call who could help? Would you do whatever it takes to feed your family and keep them safe? I know I would.

Gandhi reportedly once said, "To people who are starving, food is God." When you are in a survival mindset, the only thought you have is how to keep your family and yourself alive another day.

In 2006, Texas faced a huge prison-overpopulation problem. This was largely due to the war on drugs and incarcerating young minorities for drug-related crimes. By 2010, the prisoner population had risen 346 percent from levels in 1990. Instead of building bigger prisons, though, Texas decided to invest $241 million in programs designed to address the needs of communities, including diversion and treatment centers and recidivism-reduction programs. In the years following this investment, Texas saw massive positive effects.[18]

Journalist Ken Cuccinelli of the *National Review* wrote, "Since enacting these reforms, Texas has seen the closure of three prisons and a 25 percent reduction in its recidivism rate. Additionally, Texas taxpayers have saved nearly $3 billion in prison costs and have enjoyed their lowest rate of crime since 1968."[19]

The results in Texas foreshadow a greater change that we have the opportunity to create. Crime is often a result of a lack of opportunity. It is a cry for help. Instead of avoiding communities that have a higher crime rate, we ought to be making sure these people have resources and opportunities to succeed.

BEYOND THE SURFACE

The best way to overcome and combat this fear is by getting to know those we are afraid of. Most fearful people I meet have never done this work before. The same was true for my friend Tyler, who volunteers with our nonprofit. Tyler and his wife recently moved back to Atlanta, where they noted the need to serve those living in poverty.

"My wife has some health issues," Tyler told me. "We don't want to feel like we missed an opportunity to show some love to someone just because we're afraid of my wife's health. Of course, we have to be careful, though."

When I asked Tyler if he was ever afraid of the people he met on the streets, he responded, "Nah, man, you see, there's a tendency for people to say, 'These people are in this position because of something they did.' But when you get to know them and hear their stories, you find out it was something as simple as they lost their job, then their wife left, they have no family and nowhere to go, so they end up on the streets.

"It's crazy," Tyler continued. "It can be that quick. You look at yourself and your own life and realize how easily it could be you in the exact same position. It helps you relate.

"Maybe that's what people are really afraid of." Tyler added, "You see how easily it could have been you. There's a fear that they caused themselves to be in that place, and maybe they'll cause you or me to be in a place like that too. It's not true though."

All of the volunteers I work with who have been doing this for a while would tell you they're not afraid. They are no longer afraid because they have begun to know and connect with the people they are serving. You can't hate or fear somebody up close.

Let me be clear. Some people experiencing poverty have chosen it as a lifestyle, but most of them haven't. You won't be able to know until you hear their stories. And regarding those who have chosen this lifestyle, I challenge you to ask what real choice many of them had. In most cases, those experiencing poverty have not had a real opportunity to see what it looks like to live differently. Regardless of their choice, though, they are not monsters but rather persons with a story who do not deserve to be feared.

IMAGINE WITH ME

Think about a time you were at a networking event or a party. You're in a crowded room full of people you don't know. Rather than sitting in a corner by yourself, you decide to reach out and try to meet a few people. The first person you go up to is wearing nice clothes with their iPhone in hand. You introduce yourself, and at first it's a little awkward because meeting someone for the first time is inevitably slightly uncomfortable.

After a few minutes of conversation, though, you are both laughing, sharing stories, and talking about what you like to do in your spare time. You decide to exchange phone numbers in order to grab coffee sometime. You walk away from the encounter feeling great and excited about the new friend you've made.

A few years go by and you and your new friend lose touch. You're walking downtown one afternoon and see a homeless man pushing a shopping cart down the street. Uncomfortable and nervous, you decide to cross the street to avoid any confrontation or conversation. As you're halfway across the street, you hear the person yell your name.

"Hey! Hey . . . wait! It's me!" You turn around confused and think, *There's no way I know that guy. He doesn't look familiar.*

You turn back to continue crossing the street when this time he yells your name, "Hey! Wait up! Do you remember me?"

Even more confused, you cross back over to talk to the man who knows your name. The closer you get, you see that his clothes have holes, his beard is long and untamed, and the shopping cart is full of what looks like trash and old clothes. A few steps away you start to smell him too. He smells like he hasn't showered in weeks. You get even closer, though, and begin to recognize something about him. His eyes, face, and his voice bring you back to the event you were at a few years ago. "It's me," the homeless man says. "It's John. We met at that event. Do you remember me?"

"Of course!" you tell him. "John! I remember you now. It's been so long. How are you? What . . . happened?"

"Yeah, I mean . . ." John looks down as he continues his story. "We lost our son about two years ago, just a few months after you and I met. He was killed in a car accident. It was hard, really rough. Then my wife and I, well, she ended up leaving. After I lost her, I didn't really care about much else. I started drinking. Then I lost my job a few months after that. That didn't matter though, I had already lost everything I cared about, you know! So, here I am, I guess."

Writing the end of this story is up to you. Do you still fear the man pushing the shopping cart? Do you still cross the street or move to a different table? Do we silently drive by, afraid of a person we don't know? You decide.

Every person you see on the street, in low-income housing, living in a shelter, or experiencing poverty of any kind has a story that brought them there. I don't believe fear disappears in an instant. I believe the answer starts with how we see those experiencing poverty and homelessness and deepens as we adjust our responses toward them. We need to make daily intentional choices to live in opposition to our fear.

Ask a homeless person to tell you their story.

Talk to a coworker from a different background.

Dare to see someone who has had a tough time.

Do one thing you're normally too afraid to do.

Use this as an opportunity to intentionally disarm any fear-based living. I hope you will join me in stopping the perpetuation of fear that creates a society that cares less and less about these people. I hope you do not fear the next vulnerable and marginalized person you see but instead seek to know and understand. It starts with you really seeing people.

CHAPTER THREE

MAKING ROOM IN THE MARGINS

Last week I met with my friend Dave at a coffee shop. It had been a while since I'd seen him. He explained to me why he had been so absent lately, "After Kara and I got married a few months ago, I was starting that MBA program I told you about. At the same time, I was offered a new job, and we moved into a new house last month! I don't feel like I have time for anything. I'm barely keeping my head above water. I don't even have time to do the things I used to love doing that brought me joy. I loved serving and working with the homeless. And even going to church is getting hard."

He went on to explain that while he was physically present in a place, most of the time he was thinking about a paper he had to write, an email he had to send, or wondering what he was forgetting. This happens to all of us. Our lives fill up and we're left trying to catch up to the commitments we made.

What I found interesting about my conversation with Dave was actually the things he *didn't* say. When he described his overwhelming commitments, he left out the people and relationships in his life. Where was the time for them?

While we are fighting to make the most of every second of the margin that we do have, it's often people who pay the price for our absence. We squeeze and push every opportunity into our lives until the opportunities and commitments begin to push people outside of our reach. This affects the people we're close to (our families, friends, communities), but it also affects the people who are already being pushed out and marginalized by society. Richard Swenson, in his popular book *Margin*, says,

> We must have some room to breathe. We need freedom to think and permission to heal. Our relationships are being starved to death by velocity. No one has the time to listen, let alone love. Our children lay wounded on the ground, run over by our high-speed good intentions. Is God now pro-exhaustion? Doesn't He lead people beside the still waters anymore? Who plundered those wide-open spaces of the past, and how can we get them back? There are no fallow lands for our emotions to lie down and rest in.[1]

We live in an interconnected world. The more we collectively fill our time and margin, the more the marginalized will suffer, and the more we push people to the edges, the easier it is for them to become and stay marginalized.

Jesus told this story about a marginalized man in the New Testament,

> "A man was going down from Jerusalem to Jericho, when he was attacked by robbers. They stripped him of his clothes, beat him and went away, leaving him half dead. A priest happened to be going down the same road, and when he saw the man, he passed by on the other side. So too, a Levite, when he came to the place and saw him, passed by on the other side. But a Samaritan, as he traveled, came where the man was; and when he saw him, he took pity on him. He went to him and bandaged his

wounds, pouring on oil and wine. Then he put the man on his own donkey, brought him to an inn and took care of him. The next day he took out two denarii and gave them to the innkeeper. 'Look after him,' he said, 'and when I return, I will reimburse you for any extra expense you may have.'

"Which of these three do you think was a neighbor to the man who fell into the hands of robbers?"

The expert in the law replied, "The one who had mercy on him."

Jesus told him, "Go and do likewise." (Luke 10:30-37)

I find this story similar to our present moment in history. In the New Testament, the Levite and priest passed by for religious reasons pertaining to the Mosaic law that prohibited them from stopping. But there's not much difference between what Jesus described and what we encounter when we turn the other way at a stoplight or ignore the person begging on the subway because of our busyness or not wanting to see those who are suffering.

Our busyness can blind us to other people or at least make us feel less guilty for turning the other way and walking past someone who needs help. When we create margin, we give ourselves the opportunity to notice and truly see people. The way we spend the margin we have affects the people being pushed to the margins themselves.

MARGIN AND BUSYNESS

In our American society we seem to be moving faster and faster. Each new phone, laptop, or service promises us they're faster than the competition. *Busy* has become not just an occasional season but rather the default setting for our everyday lives. We celebrate busy and look down on the alternative, idleness. But this busyness creates a cycle we're trapped in. Richard Swenson unpacks more of this from his book *Margin*, "We have more 'things per person' than any other nation in history. Closets are full, storage space is used up, and cars can't fit into garages. Having first imprisoned us with debt, possessions then take over our houses and occupy our time. This begins to sound like an invasion. Everything I own owns me. Why would I want more?"[2]

It's a common response to the question "How are you?" "Oh, you know, good, busy-busy." Not many people will respond, "Ah, good, just spent a few days relaxing. I really haven't done much lately." But why?

In recent years, research has shown that busyness is a new status symbol. Experiments have shown that people associate busyness with high status. Interestingly enough, it comes from the idea of achieving the American dream. The general population believes that we live in a society where hard work equals success for everybody.[3]

Busyness can also add to internal poverty as we try to add things to our lives in unhealthy ways in order to feel more accepted and loved and more at *home*, where most of us long to be. This spiritual poverty can cause us to pursue meaning through activity rather than finding it in being created by a God who cares for us.

Is it true? Does busyness mean success? What is success? The success they're talking about here is mainly monetary. The things that currently keep us busy and occupy most of our time do not necessarily give us purpose or leave a legacy.

Watching someone choose busyness over people is painful. It hits a deep vein in the stories we tell ourselves about who we are and what we are worth. Can you imagine a time when someone told you they were too busy for you? When someone chose the pursuit of material things over the pursuit of a relationship with another person? We do it all the time. We forget the consequences of telling people they are worth less than a trophy or a number in a bank.

What messages do we send people when we tell them they are not important enough for our time or to be seen? What are we chasing with that time instead? We end up with people who are overcommitted, burned out, and fighting for acclaim and possessions that fade. Before we know it, we are committed to things we never cared about in the first place. It's the father looking back after years of fighting to provide everything for his family who realizes that maybe his kids just wanted extra time with him.

We accumulate cars and houses, watch the numbers in our bank account fluctuate (and hopefully rise), and trade our time to make it happen. It's funny—we begin to believe that the busier we are, the bigger impact we're making, and that somehow constant movement must mean we're moving forward in life. We've become good at fooling ourselves. We begin to live in a society where "I'm too busy for you" becomes the norm, and we are taught and teach others that people are not valuable.

When Jesus came to earth, though, he clearly preached a different message. He often communicated messages that went against how society and culture teach us to operate.

In fact, he said real treasures and worth come from investing in the things of God over the things that we accumulate. He concluded that the things we store on earth will leave us and fade, but the intangible things we assign to God will endure.

> Do not store up for yourselves treasures on earth, where moths and vermin destroy, and where thieves break in and steal. But store up for yourselves treasures in heaven, where moths and vermin do not destroy, and where thieves do not break in and steal. For where your treasure is, there your heart will be also. (Matthew 6:19-21)

Jesus knew that addressing inner spiritual poverty brought the greatest type of freedom. His words still ring true today. Our joy is not in striving to obtain but is found in maintaining a relationship with God Almighty.

I've had to be careful of the temptation to let work and busyness control my own life. I often find myself on the road, traveling to speak. There are two general mantras I have about life as it pertains to this and the time I have to make an impact. The first is that anyone can make a difference. And the second is that I won't live forever. The idea that I won't live forever scares me and at the same time comforts me. It reminds me that the only things I can take with me are the relationships and impact I've made and left behind.

It took me a long time to come to that realization and even longer to actually decide what things are worth spending my time investing in. Within that process, I discovered that finding margin in my life for the things I care about and prioritization go hand in hand.

We have to define our core values. This might seem strange, especially as a Christian. Aren't our core values defined for us already? They must be those rules and ideals outlined in the Bible. Few Christians I have met, though, are able to separate the words from the Bible into tangible, actionable rhythms that permeate their lives. There are questions you must ask yourself and answer on your own.

- What do you stand for?
- What makes you mad?
- What keeps you up at night?
- What worries you?
- What do your family and marriage stand for?

Once you have the answers to these, you will be able to build a foundation of what you stand for and what you will give your time to. These sorts of things serve as guardrails. If there were no lines on the highway, people would drive all over the place, getting into accidents. That's what happens with our lives. We don't have things in place to guide where we want to go; we're too easily sidetracked.

When asked what the greatest commandment was, Jesus said, "'Love the Lord your God with all your heart and with all your soul and with all your mind.' This is the first and greatest commandment. And the second is like it: 'Love your neighbor as yourself.' All the Law and the Prophets hang on these two commandments" (Matthew 22:37-40).

What does that mean for the way you spend your time and how you value things?

Our core values will inform our priorities. And that's what we end up giving time, money, and resources to. I'll never forget teaching my daughter and son our family's core values. I told them we love God, we love family, we love people, and we do our best at whatever work we put our hands to in this life.

I know this sounds simple, but it is amazing to see my children value spending time with our family and serving with my wife and me. It was even greater watching them both take a step to be baptized, and I got to be the one that did it! We have tried to teach our children that there is no separation between how we live for God and what we do for God.

In fact, our living with and for God should show up in our lives because it becomes a part of who we are. Therefore, serving and making time to help other people is not punishment for my kids. It flows out of our set of core values as believers.

MY OWN MARGIN

One of my biggest dreams is to have "Dr." in front of my name. Why? I was a high school dropout and went on to obtain four degrees. I overcame what many people thought would take me out. I thought it would be awesome to go from least likely to succeed to being Dr. Terence. Because I highly value education, and as someone who once had odds stacked against him, getting a PhD was and is an important goal I've always had.

I can still remember the day I dropped out of school. I was close to eighteen and about to graduate. The voices of teachers who told me I would never make it, that I would never amount to anything, still ring in my head.

The pursuit of my doctorate was a sort of symbolic shift for me. I wanted to prove to myself and others that I had what it took. I wanted to gain the knowledge I needed to be able to help others. The degree seemed like the most important piece of paper I could ever hold.

In 2011 I started a doctoral program. Around the same time, I was working with those experiencing poverty and thinking what it would be like to pursue this work of bringing awareness and reconciliation to these people full-time.

I spoke to a mentor about my concerns related to pursuing both things at the same time, and he challenged me, "You're going to school and you have some experiences from the classroom, but I think you could get a lot more experience if you fully immersed yourself in the community."

I knew exactly what he meant. It was one thing to theorize and learn about poverty and biblical theology while sitting at a desk; it's another to get out on the streets in order to know the people and pursue solutions.

It quickly became clear that getting my doctorate was something I wanted to do for myself. It's a good and important goal, but it wasn't the right time. The work and the people in front of me needed my attention more than the classroom did.

I was two classes into the degree when I told my wife, "I think I'm going to stop the program."

It was difficult to give up this dream, but I saw it as a necessary sacrifice to store up treasure in heaven. I know now, though, that it was without a doubt the best decision I could have made. I would rather be closer to those we are serving than have a professor stand in front of me in a big classroom and tell me about things he may never have done. There's a big difference.

And the lessons I'm learning from my work include indispensable knowledge I couldn't get anywhere else.

I still desire a PhD. Should I keep putting it off? If the time is right, the opportunity will be created for me, but until then I can't let my personal pursuits rise above people.

A PhD is a good thing. Sometimes we have to give up good things to make space in our lives for even more important things. This is where knowing our core values comes into play. We have a limited amount of time, space, and resources to allocate to different things. It starts with recognizing what we're doing with our time and resources now in order to move to a rhythm that fits our values and God's plan for our lives. Who knows, I may end up creating enough margin to complete that degree, but as of right now, reaching people is more of a priority. And I am thankful because I still get a chance to lecture in colleges, universities, and so many other places where I can use all of my education.

YOUR MARGIN

How can you begin to create margin in your own life? When I think about margin, I think about reducing life to its simplest form. How much do any of us really need?

Most of what we're chasing rusts, rots, fades, and deteriorates with time. We can't take our PhD diplomas to the grave; nor can we take our big screen TVs, iPhones, or credit cards.

A few years ago I was introduced to the president of a prestigious movie studio. He learned about my march to Washington, DC, and followed the journey on social media. He emailed my wife and told her that he wanted to sit down with me when I got back.

We set up a time, and I drove up to the gated building and told the guard who I was invited to meet with. His eyes narrowed, confused, he looked at his computer, then at me, and back at his computer. Slowly the gate began to open, and I drove to the front of the studios.

I walked into the front door and was greeted by the receptionist, who led me to an elevator set to go directly to the top floor. I started to put the pieces together that the man I was meeting was actually *the* president of the entire company.

The elevator opened to an office with floor-to-ceiling windows and a view of the entire city. We sat down and talked about the March Against Poverty and what led me to walk over seven hundred miles to bring attention to the poor. I began to tell him my story, about my childhood, watching my mother and family struggle with poverty, and the time I had spent homeless. Tears welled up in his eyes, which he quickly blinked away.

"I want to help. What can I do?" Surprised by his immediate offer, I thought of the next program the organization was doing, "Well, we do something called Wishlist Christmas. A campaign to give presents to people we already know and to fill needs in the community we're serving."

He and his wife and brother bought all the gifts on the list we sent him. And close to Christmas, he brought his family to volunteer with us. There he was—a prestigious movie producer—standing next to me giving gifts to families struggling with poverty.

He turned to me that day and said, "We need this. My family needs more of this." Since then, he communicated that serving would be a part of their lifestyle. If someone like that can pause and create the space to serve, can't the rest of us, who are comparably less busy and responsible for much less, find margin to do the same?

I often suggest that people start small, even one hour a month. Does that sound reasonable? I guarantee anyone can find and dedicate one hour a month.

"But what if I only have an hour? Or $5 per month to contribute? Is it even worth it?" I hear this a lot too.

An hour a week isn't a lot for one person. What we miss, though, is that this fight is not solved by one individual but through our combined efforts. What if one thousand people reading this dedicated one hour a month? In one year that's twelve thousand hours dedicated to providing opportunities and creating relationships with one another to fight for justice.

Just last week I was at our center when a car pulled into our lot. We had just finished our morning program and ran out of bags of food. An older woman got out from the car and made her way to the lobby. She shared part of her story with us, "I'm eighty-three years old. I've got cancer and don't want to have any more surgeries. If I go—I just go. I have my grandson in the car, and he's out of school for the summer. I don't have enough to feed him now that he's out of school." The woman started tearing up, and I was running through how we could help this woman even though we had just run out of groceries.

At the same time, another car pulled into our center and a volunteer got out of her car, opened her trunk, pulled out bags of groceries, and dropped them off as donations. We immediately directed the volunteer to help put the donated food in the grandmother's car, and grandma burst into tears.

It took the volunteer twenty-five minutes to drive to our center and only a few minutes to round up the food in her pantry to donate. Less than an hour of time helped feed a family. No matter how small the act is, it matters. Impact starts one person at a time.

I sometimes wonder what it would look like if Christians started the revolution—the revolution of being generous with our time and creating margin for things that matter. A recent study says there are around 240 million Christians in the United States.[4] Can you imagine if 240 million Christians donated an hour each month to further the message of Jesus by serving the poor and standing up for the voiceless? We could change the world.

You might say giving someone something will not eliminate a huge problem like poverty. However, I'm not advocating for people to receive free things and for others to give so they feel good about themselves. I'm calling for more than that, for a revolution and radical change in our priorities. I'm advocating for people to realize how much of an impact we could have if we spent more time with people—serving, seeing, and loving those on the margins of society.

It takes bravery to stand up to the lives we're living and change. Often it means we must let go of something else we're doing. Maybe it's even something good. It starts with an introspective look at our own values and then at how those values permeate our lives.

What if we spent all that time building up people instead of building up bigger storehouses for all our possessions? How would the world change if we made margin to serve the vulnerable, marginalized, and voiceless? Wasn't that the side Jesus was on?

CHAPTER FOUR

HOW MUCH IS ENOUGH?

During my week of experiencing homelessness, my friends and I stood on the street corner asking for spare change as cars flew by. Hundreds of cars passed by us in the four hours I stood there. The worst part was when someone ignored us completely, as if we didn't even exist. When we weren't on the corner, my friends and I would walk under the bridge to rest. Other times we'd walk miles to the closest McDonald's, hoping someone would buy us something off the dollar menu.

A lot goes on in a person's mind, standing out there. How did I get here? Who will help? How will I eat? Will this next car stop? Do they see us?

Other days we'd walk down to the homeless shelter to see if there was any room left. Depending on the day of the week, we'd walk to the nearest food pantry or soup kitchen. In this constant drifting I wondered, *Who is responsible for the poor?*

Was it the people in the cars driving past? Were the non-profits and shelters responsible? Or is it the government's job to make sure the poor aren't starving to death on the streets? How do we become people who not only accept responsibility for the destitute but also shift our focus from being self-centered to other-centered?

Now that I run a nonprofit that's dedicated to working with the impoverished, I hear a lot of different replies to these questions. Everyone has a different answer for who exactly is responsible for the poor. (Hint: people rarely say it's themselves.) How did Jesus respond to this question?

In Matthew 25 Jesus says,

> Then the King will say to those on his right, "Come, you who are blessed by my Father; take your inheritance, the kingdom prepared for you since the creation of the world. For I was hungry, and you gave me something to eat, I was thirsty and you gave me something to drink, I was a stranger and you invited me in, I needed clothes and you clothed me, I was sick and you looked after me, I was in prison and you came to visit me."
>
> Then these righteous will answer him, "Lord, when did we see you hungry and feed you, or thirsty and give you something to drink? When did we see you a stranger and invite you in, or needing clothes and clothe you? When did we see you sick or in prison and go to visit you?"
>
> And the King will reply, "Truly I tell you, whatever you did for one of the least of these brothers and sisters of mine, you did it for me."
>
> Then he will say to those on his left, "Depart from me, you who are cursed, into the eternal fire prepared for the devil and his angels. For I was hungry and you gave me nothing to eat, I was thirsty and you gave me nothing to drink, I was a stranger and you did not invite me in, I needed clothes and you did not clothe me, I was sick and in prison and you did not look after me."
>
> They also will answer, "Lord, when did we see you hungry or thirsty or a stranger or needing clothes or sick or in prison, and did not help you?"

He will reply, "Truly I tell you, whatever you did not do for one of the least of these, you did not do for me." (Matthew 25:34-45)

When I read this passage, its meaning is obvious. Simple, actually. It's tempting to overcomplicate it. I believe, though, that it means we Christians are the first in line to care for the poor.

It's easy for Christians to make excuses about why people are poor and, worse, believe the false narratives we have been fed through media or uninformed people. Sometimes we use Scripture wrongly to justify our distance and apathy toward the poor. I have heard Matthew 26:11—"the poor you will always have with you"— misquoted many times to excuse people for not helping the poor. When Jesus makes this statement, he's actually suggesting doing two things. He's quoting another passage (Deuteronomy 15:11), and he's teaching a disciple the importance of serving the poor.

If you were around Jesus, who is Jewish, and understood the context, you'd know exactly what he meant.[1] Here's the original passage to consider,

If there is among you anyone in need, a member of your community in any of your towns within the land that the Lord your God is giving you, do not be hard-hearted or tight-fisted toward your needy neighbor. You should rather open your hand, willingly lending enough to meet the need, whatever it may be. Be careful that you do not entertain a mean thought, thinking, "The seventh year, the year of remission, is near," and therefore view your needy neighbor with hostility and give nothing; your neighbor might cry to the Lord against you, and you would incur guilt. Give liberally and be ungrudging when you do so, for on this account the Lord your God will bless you in all your work and in all that you undertake. Since there will never cease to be some in need on the earth, I therefore command you, "Open your hand to the poor and needy neighbor in your land." (Deuteronomy 15:7-11 NRSV)

Therefore, when we read the words in context, the command is for us to be openhanded toward the poor and not apathetic or distant. In the Gospel of John, where this phrase is found, Jesus is actually saying that we should be generous toward those who are poor. In fact, when we read these words found in John 12, Jesus is rebuking his disciple Judas (who was greedy and a thief) for being contemptuous toward a woman for pouring her perfume on Jesus.

Then Mary took about a pint of pure nard, an expensive perfume; she poured it on Jesus' feet and wiped his feet with her hair. And the house was filled with the fragrance of the perfume.

But one of his disciples, Judas Iscariot, who was later to betray him, objected, "Why wasn't this perfume sold and the money given to the poor? It was worth a year's wages." He did not say this because he cared about the poor but because he was a thief; as keeper of the money bag, he used to help himself to what was put into it.

"Leave her alone," Jesus replied. "It was intended that she should save this perfume for the day of my burial. You will always have the poor among you, but you will not always have me." (John 12:3-8)

GOOD NEWS TO THE BROKEN

I remember when I first paid attention the gospel message. I'd gone to church growing up, but like most kids I hadn't made the faith my own until I was in my twenties. At the time I was headed down a destructive path, and the good news of the gospel helped turn my life around. What shocked me is it's based on a sort of lack—a lack of access to God. We carry spiritual poverty and need someone else to pay that debt, which of course is what Jesus did.

I have always defined poverty as a lack of access. So as Christians, shouldn't we realize how great it is to be given access to something we so desperately need? If that's what the gospel is, why are we so hesitant to take responsibility for the poor in return?

As I mentioned earlier, the apostle Paul writes that Jesus became poor so we could have spiritual wealth in relationship with God. Paul says Jesus gave up everything. David Jones observes, "In order to take on human flesh and dwell among sinful people and the filth of this world, Jesus had to set aside the wealth of heaven."[2] Jesus "emptied himself, by taking the form of a servant, being born in the likeness of men. And being found in human form, he humbled himself by becoming obedient to the point of death, even death on a cross" (Philippians 2:7-8 ESV).

One of the largest barriers I've found to this is the distinction Christians make between orthodoxy versus orthopraxy. *Orthodoxy* focuses on making sure we're thinking right about God. *Orthopraxy*, on the other hand, focuses on how the doctrine is actually practiced.

The greatest way to show people what you believe is to display it in how you live.

OUR MODERN GREED

The opposite of a lack of access is the pursuit of abundance. The pursuit of abundance is otherwise known as greed. Greed is difficult to discuss. It's a big, ugly word, and most people wouldn't admit to being greedy. Most of us don't know that we're personally fighting greed.

Many things are marketed to our greed and our willingness to get all we can out of life. Buy this and you will go further; purchase that and you will succeed. Live here. Shop there. Madison Avenue tells us it's okay to accumulate all that we can without any thought or concern for others. Greed has contributed to the inner poverty we face in so many ways.

Henri J. M. Nouwen, a well-known priest and author who lived the last days of his life pastoring people living with disabilities, learned we are all impoverished in some way. But when we choose to give our lives, we discover that there is even a blessing in our poverty. Nouwen writes in *Bread for the Journey,*

> How can we embrace poverty as a way to God when everyone around us wants to become rich? Poverty has many forms. We have to ask ourselves: "What is my poverty?" Is it lack of money, lack of emotional stability, lack of a loving partner, lack of security, lack of safety, lack of self-confidence? Each human being has a place of poverty. That's the place where God wants to dwell! "How blessed are the poor," Jesus says (Matthew 5:3). This means that our blessing is hidden in our poverty. We are so inclined to cover up our poverty and ignore it that we often miss the opportunity to discover God, who dwells in it. Let's dare to see our poverty as the land where our treasure is hidden.[3]

What if instead of viewing our own inner poverty as a place to run from, we start to view it as a place where God wants to meet us? Then we can use this perspective to love others who are also poor in some way. However, we must first let go of the greed that is creating our inner emptiness.

When Adam and Eve were in the Garden, the snake tempted them by convincing them there was something more—that they could know more, be more—if they just ate the fruit. This is a temptation that plagues you and me today. How might I trade a fraction of God for something a little more tangible?

We curate a false sense of belonging by collecting possessions of perceived value. Having more stuff than our neighbor must mean we're more important, that we belong. The greed perpetuates the deep void, the search for acceptance, and our desperation to find worth. When we search for our meaning in the pursuit of more over our pursuit of God, we damage our own souls. Greed teaches us to look out for ourselves until we're blind to the needs of those right next to us. Greed even teaches us to pursue the creation over our Creator.

Isn't it funny how people are in pursuit of everything but the one who created us all?

It's deep in our society. It's why someone bought the buildings right behind the Atlanta homeless shelter that was closed to build three-hundred-thousand-dollar lofts.[4] It's why the health care industry and the prison system are for-profit. We live in an economy that thrives by trading people for profit. It trickles into our schools, our churches, and our families. This is why neighborhoods succumb to gentrification and people are pushed out of their communities.

For you and me, greed looks more like upgrading our phones every time a new model comes out, having an expensive car, and buying a bigger house. I have been guilty of this too. Something about getting that next "thing" gives us a temporary rush that makes us forget about anything worthwhile. If you ask me, in many ways capitalistic greed has driven us away from the basic foundation of loving people. People are no longer the focus; more stuff is.

Jesus gave us a story for how to engage greed. In Luke he told this parable of the rich fool:

> He said to them, "Watch out! Be on your guard against all kinds of greed; life does not consist in an abundance of possessions."
>
> And he told them this parable: "The ground of a certain rich man yielded an abundant harvest. He thought to himself, 'What shall I do? I have no place to store my crops.'
>
> "Then he said, 'This is what I'll do. I will tear down my barns and build bigger ones, and there I will store my surplus grain. And I'll say to myself, "You have plenty of grain laid up for many years. Take life easy; eat, drink and be merry."'
>
> "But God said to him, 'You fool! This very night your life will be demanded from you. Then who will get what you have prepared for yourself?'
>
> "This is how it will be with whoever stores up things for themselves but is not rich toward God." (Luke 12:15-21)

The question rephrased goes something like this, "If you died tomorrow, what have you worked your whole life for? Will it all disappear? What have you really worked for?"

It's a sobering question, but an important one. Rarely do we spend time imagining what happens to all of our stuff when we die. Combating our greed begins with taking responsibility for those around us.

YOU CAN DO MORE THAN YOU THINK

I was talking with Andrea a few months ago. She wanted to get involved with the work we're doing in Atlanta. She started by saying, "I'd love to help, but I just don't know if I can. I don't have a lot of extra money right now. Making ends meet is tough. I don't know what I can do."

Rarely do rich people make huge financial contributions to our ministry. Sure, that kind of giving looks good on social media, but rarely is an impact made by few people with large monetary donations. The sort of change we're making is a societal one where we come together and share our skills to provide access and opportunity for everyone.

As we got to know Andrea more, we discovered she was good at researching. At the same time, we were helping one of our friends, Brian, transition from homelessness to stability after ten years. Brian's story was a relatable one, the kind you realize could happen to any of us. He lost his job during the Great Recession, his wife left him, and he turned to alcohol to self-medicate. Eventually, he found himself living on the streets.

One day we found Brian digging through our dumpster looking for food. After a couple months of working with him, he met Andrea, who wasn't sure how she could help. The two talked for a while, and the more this volunteer heard Brian's story, the more questions she asked about him and his family. Andrea helped him research and track down some of the family he had lost touch with. After a few weeks of research and reaching out, she was able to help connect him with his family and his daughter he hadn't spoken to in over thirty years. She was able to see them reunited. And these connections helped give Brian the motivation and support to escape poverty, find a sustainable job, and start his life over again.

This is why we need you. This is why we need everyone.

Some people love paperwork. Others can build. Some of you can design and decorate. The more people who get involved and use their skills, the bigger the team of people who can make a difference.

When Paul wrote about the body of Christ (1 Corinthians 12:12-27), this is what I imagine he thought it could look like. The eye needs the hand. The head needs the feet. God has given the body of Christ different gifts so we can work together to imitate Christ. God will gain glory from the body as it functions as a healthy whole. And the world is changed as we do it.

THE IMPACT WE HAVE

I'd like to leave you with one more story.

Last week I took my son to the barber shop. It's one of those sacred father-son traditions I hope he carries on if he has a son. While we were there, my wife and daughter walked to the nearby Macy's in the mall. My son and I finished our haircuts and started walking toward the car to wait for the girls to come back. In the parking lot I saw a man with his two children. They were sitting on the curb, and I couldn't help but wonder what they were doing there. I didn't know this man's story but I couldn't get rid of the image of him and his kids in that parking lot. I wondered who he was, what brought him here, and if he had the same opportunities I had.

You see, I wouldn't be who I am today without the relationships in my life that brought me here. I grew up in a single-parent household—just my mom, my sister, and me. My mom worked multiple jobs to provide for us. Her struggle with poverty and the lack of a father figure in my life left me to wrestle with my own identity. What it meant to be a man with character and integrity was foreign to me. I learned what it meant to father myself through a lot of situations in my teen years. I ended up running the streets with my friends. I lived in parks and out of the trunk of my car. Most people who look at me now would never guess that I had joined a gang and was locked up a few times.

I was twenty years old the day I decided to make a change in my life. At the time, I was sitting on a cold metal bench in a dark jail cell.

An older man next to me in the cell turned to me and said, "Why you wasting your life?"

Something deep in me heard him, like, really heard him. There was this intangible but certain potential I knew I had to do something with in my life. And it was the same potential I saw in the man sitting on the curb of the parking lot.

My mom picked me up from jail and the charges were dropped. My life was never the same. From there I met hundreds of people who influenced me, making me the man I am now. I would not be where I am had it not been for relationships and the exposure I had.

Sometimes we don't see the importance of how exposure can change somebody's world. I've been in rooms with CEOs and lawyers and speaking to crowds of thousands. I wonder if the guy in the parking lot will have the opportunity to meet the people I've met. So who am I to store my opportunities, influence, or connections and boast that I am a self-made man?

There is no such thing as the self-made person. We're all products of our environments, connections, and access to opportunity. The responsibility is a collective one. No one person, one group, or one church has the singular answer. It's like trying to solve a puzzle with missing pieces that are hiding under the table because they don't see themselves as part of the greater picture.

If the man sitting in the parking lot with his kids isn't exposed to opportunities, will his children be? Maybe, if they're lucky. Do my children deserve greater opportunities because their father was afforded them? Do those children deserve them any less?

It's not about pursuing poverty as a goal either. It's about using the resources, skills, and opportunities we have as tools to work together and enhance each others' lives. It's a shift in our hearts and minds to take responsibility for not just the tangible things we have but for all the resources we have been awarded. We're working together to fight against greed and to fight for one another as a glimpse into the kingdom of God.

What does that mean for you? Think back to the ways the sacrifice and care of others have given you opportunities that changed your life. How can you become someone who sees others as opportunities and not burdens?

CHAPTER FIVE

IGNORANCE CAN BE HURTFUL

Once a month I head downtown with a group of volunteers to serve and get to know the community that's struggling to make ends meet. The volunteers come from a variety of local churches or they have seen our work on social media, and everyone comes from diverse backgrounds. We call this service opportunity "Gather Atlanta" because people come together from all walks of life to serve those who are overlooked in society. We've learned that service can unite people from different ethnic groups, and this honors God. Years ago, my wife and I started taking groups onto the streets to create an opportunity for people to take the love of God beyond the four walls of the church. It's easy to become inward focused and forget what's happening outside the church (assuming you are not a part of a community that makes serving a priority).

However, we are well aware that it's sometimes hard to make sure every volunteer has been through the appropriate training; we want to serve everyone.

One morning a few of us were setting up tables and putting out resources when a volunteer, Anna, began to lay out some food she had brought with her to distribute. Anna pulled out ham and cheese sandwiches, a fairly normal and easy meal to give away.

A group of people started to gather next to the tables, and we started to distribute the food, water, hygiene kits, and the like.

An older man came up to the woman with the sandwiches and asked, "What sort of meat is in the sandwiches?"

"Ham and cheese. Why does that concern you? Take the bag." Anna said in a belittling tone.

"Oh, okay. No thank you. I don't want that today." The older man answered.

"What? Excuse me?" her disbelief and anger apparent. She continued, "I can't *believe* how ungrateful some people can be. That's ridiculous!"

I watched the scene unfold and walked over to the older man who had refused the sandwich to find out why he didn't want the food. After a minute of conversation, I discovered that he was diabetic and had just become vegan, committing himself to eat more vegetables.

He told me his family had a history of health problems and that from living on the streets he had gotten used to eating a lot of the unhealthy, cheaper foods that are handed out. He explained that he was trying to get his health in a better place so he could live a better life.

We all act like Anna a lot more than we'd probably like to admit. We let our ignorance influence our reactions. *Ignorance* is one of those words. It's got a negative connotation and is often used as a synonym for *stupid and closed-minded.*

But from what I've seen, ignorance looks more like the inability to understand or share the feelings of others. Ignorance is defined as simply a lack of knowledge and information, but it's what we do in reaction when we are faced with our own ignorance that makes all the difference. The trap I've seen most people get into is believing the way they see the world is the only way the world exists, that what they see and experience is *the* truth.

WHERE DOES IGNORANCE COME FROM?

Almost all of us have some holiday traditions—matching pajamas, a Christmas tree, the ceramic manger scene, or maybe one of those Advent calendars with chocolates behind each day's door. In my family we started serving as a tradition. Serving simply means finding a place to volunteer or creating our own volunteer opportunity for service, which is a core value of our family during the Advent season.

My wife and I decided many years ago, before we had children, that we would place *being a gift* as a top priority before we opened any gifts with our children. Even before our children entered the world, we set the tone by doing this every single year.

For the last fourteen years, we've taken a group of people to serve those living on the streets. This includes anything from sharing hot soup to sitting and talking with someone who has no family and is experiencing homelessness. Or it could be passing out blankets to those who have to endure the cold winter weather. Now our kids join us in these activities.

Of course, this sacrifice hasn't always been easy in the face of consumerism, which suggests Christmas is all about ourselves and purchasing every new gadget. But my wife and I are steadfast in wanting to teach our children early that it's greater to share and be a tangible blessing to other people who do not have as much.

So each Christmas we wake up early, brush our teeth, put on clothes, and head downtown to find people in the cold and give them warm items. It does our hearts good to see our children participating in this practice that we believe honors God. In fact, one of my favorite passages is found in Proverbs 14:31: "Whoever is kind to the needy honors God."

Researchers from Northeastern University found that up to 93 percent of our future actions are predictable based on our past.[1] We follow traditions and customs because they make us feel safer. We go along with and do what everyone else is doing to avoid pain and loneliness. Most of the time we do things because it's the way we've always done things. That's not necessarily a bad thing unless it has consequences for people who don't have a say in the matter. When our actions and traditions hurt other people, or when we don't recognize the people we're excluding in the midst of what we're doing, that's when our ignorance comes into play.

Most of the time ignorance comes from beliefs or preconceived notions passed down or overheard or created from another generation and from history. The good thing about this, though, is that as soon as we're open to questioning where a set of beliefs or actions came from, we're halfway to solving the problem.

So what do we believe about the poor now? How are the poor perceived? In most cases, people believe the poor are lazy, uneducated, dangerous, problems, without character, deserving of their poverty, and so on. We've seen these perceptions in the news, in comments from people we look up to, and from our own worldview. In the article "Busting the Myth of 'Welfare Makes People Lazy,'" Derek Thompson writes, "the notion is buried so deep within mainstream political thought that it can often be stated without evidence."[2]

We sometimes think, *I work hard at my job so I don't have to beg on the streets. Isn't it the same for these people?* (That's often not the case. The consequences of systemic injustice almost always have a part in these conversations.)

Did you know that people experiencing homelessness often have to burn donated clothes like firewood to stay warm while living outside? And the fastest-growing population of homeless individuals is families with children?[3]

I could ask myself these questions and complicate the issue a hundred times. It's my tendency to try to figure out all the details and educate myself on all the facts. But in the end, I (and we) must get back to the root of our beliefs and ask, How does God see the poor? And then measure ourselves against that standard.

THE GOD WHO SEES

So how does God see the poor? In Genesis, Hagar, a marginalized, poor, Egyptian servant girl, cried out to God in her desperation. Hagar was running away when an angel of the Lord appeared to her and asked where she was going. After being seen in her darkest moment by God, Hagar "gave this name to the LORD who spoke to her: 'You are the God who sees me,' for she said, 'I have now seen the One who sees me'" (Genesis 16:13).

God restores dignity to Hagar by seeing her—seeing where she was, where she was going, why she was afraid, and calling her into her greater identity. God is the original one who says, "I see you." He says it to you and me in our darkest moments, and to the poor and marginalized on the street. If we are followers of the God who sees, then we too must become people who see. We must become people who show and tell others, "I see you."

The Bible has over two thousand references to poverty and justice. The following are a few of the most relevant to consider.

The LORD is a refuge for the oppressed,
  a stronghold in times of trouble. (Psalm 9:9)

Blessed are you who are poor,
  for yours is the kingdom of God.
Blessed are you who hunger now,
  for you will be satisfied.
Blessed are you who weep now,
  for you will laugh. (Luke 6:20-21)

No one should seek their own good, but the good of others.
(1 Corinthians 10:24)

Share your belongings with your needy fellow Christians,
and open your homes to strangers. (Romans 12:13 GNT)

If a brother or sister is poorly clothed and lacking in daily
food, and one of you says to them, "Go in peace, be warmed
and filled," without giving them the things needed for the
body, what good is that? (James 2:15-16 ESV)

Jesus always asks us to sacrifice.

He constantly asks us to care for the poor and the marginalized. In church, we make it complicated by creating special
service days or making excuses for why the poor are in that situation. Unfortunately, though, when we neglect the poor we are
missing the core of the gospel. We miss it completely. We're
focused on the wrong things. Loving those who are oppressed
and outcast is at the core of the gospel.

I asked my friend Brenton, a pastor in Virginia, what changed
his view about the poor, and he gave me some perceptive
thoughts on what it looked like to grow up in a church that
never talked about the poor.

He explained, "It was never something we were taught. The
focus of our discipleship and growth as a Christian was
always centered on achieving a certain level of morality. It

was always about what you do and don't drink, who you do and don't spend time with, what you watched on TV, and your sexual ethics."

He continued, "We never understood what a social ethic looks like and only focused on personal piety. That meant never understanding or being taught what Jesus' ethics for the poor looked like. That's what it was like growing up in the conservative, evangelical bread-basket church."

I asked my friend what his transition looked like. He said, "It wasn't necessarily a switch in one moment. It looked a lot like being around a community of people who were really living it out. It also looked like meeting and getting to know the stories of the people that the 'social justice' issues were affecting. I had to ask hard questions about why we were doing what we were doing. Jesus never strayed from asking the hard question or telling the 'best' religious people they were missing the point."

We're tasked with doing the same. We no longer have the excuse to be ignorant of the needs and ails of the poor and how paramount caring for them is. Caring for and relating to the poor is the gospel. It parallels Jesus coming to earth to do what we couldn't do on our own. If we miss or don't fully understand the mercy that's been extended to us, it won't transform our lives the way it needs to.

We're missing the point—striving after artificial holiness instead of demonstrating love to someone the way Jesus loved us. It can be difficult to take the focus off ourselves as the heroes and martyrs we've become in our pursuit of holiness. Many of us have worked our whole lives for this. But what is it worth if we've missed the point?

FROM IGNORANCE TO EMPATHY

When a lawyer asked Jesus how he could inherit the kingdom of God, Jesus replied with the story of the good Samaritan. We've talked about this story and how it relates to our responsibility toward the poor, but it relates to our ignorance too. It starts with a man traveling on the road to Jericho, who is attacked, robbed, beaten half to death, and left on the side of the road. First, a priest passes by and crosses the road to avoid him. Then a Levite, another religious man, crosses the road to avoid the beaten man. Last, a Samaritan, an enemy of the Jews, comes across the traveler. Instead of passing by, he aids the man, brings him into the nearest city, and pays for his recovery.

Why did Jesus tell this story? What did it mean? I've studied the passage over and over, and something stuck out to me about the Samaritan. In those days, the Jews hated the Samaritans, and in fact, depending on what region they were in, many Samaritans were oppressed and discriminated against. What was going on inside the Samaritan's head? Was he just some incredibly noble man passing by?

The more I researched how Samaritans were treated at that time, the more I came to realize that this Samaritan probably knew what it was like to be beaten and left on the side of the road. He knew what it meant to be hated, ignored, and treated as if he were worth less than everyone else. Something happens in us when we experience something firsthand. It changes the way we see, react to, and understand the world. Empathy develops in ways that transform us. Real transformation happens when we are able to acknowledge our own biases against people who look and experience life differently.

I experienced something like this when I was homeless. When I was growing up, my family (led by my mom) experienced periods when we moved from one house to another and struggled financially, but we were never acutely homeless for an extended period of time.

As an adult, I chose to be homeless to experience the realities faced by the people I was serving and working with. Though I thought I understood much about being on the streets, standing in the cold under a bridge, hungry, and feeling ashamed I couldn't buy my own dinner was different from anything I've ever known. It's more than I can fully explain. Experiencing the feelings, the thoughts, the doubts, and the fears was much more intense, frustrating, and frightening than I could have imagined.

Those moments and subsequent ones have been instrumental in developing empathy and understanding toward a group of people I thought I knew a lot about. When Jesus came to earth to experience life with us, he wanted us to know that he understood, he was here, and his compassion was shared because he was in the midst of the chaos with us.

COMBATING IGNORANCE

Back to the story of Anna and the ham sandwiches. After I talked to the man who turned down the sandwiches and heard about his diabetes and trying to create a healthier lifestyle, I also spoke to Anna. I told her the man's story, that he was diabetic and was desperately trying to make a positive change in his life.

Her entire attitude changed; she was moved to tears by his story. Something happened in her when she was exposed to his world. The homeless person you pass at the intersection has a story too. After encounters like Anna's, we become responsible for our potential ignorance and our lives will be changed.

Having an open mindset and being willing to ask questions is the first step in combating the things we don't know. This looks like more than the outward actions of donating food and passing out sandwiches. It's about hearing someone's story and being able to relate to it. These people's stories are littered with pain and hard times, but also with love and family. You will connect to pieces of their stories if you allow yourself space.

After the willingness to combat ignorance comes exposure to things we are uncertain of. Whenever there's a slight feeling of uncertainty, fear, or confusion about something or someone, stop before you react, and ask for the rest of the story. Exposing yourself to someone else's worldview will strengthen yours, and the conversation and relationship will help you relate to someone the way Jesus did.

The only way to get rid of darkness is to let light in. Create relationships with people who aren't like you, and you will learn the stories, the pain, and the most beautiful parts of other people's lives. The only way to connect with one another is to seek to understand rather than to react out of our preconceptions about someone or something.

DIGNITY MUSEUM

One of our latest projects involves converting a forty-foot shipping container into Atlanta's first museum to represent homelessness and poverty. There are no spaces that focus on educating the general public about the realities the homeless live with in society and sharing their stories. We are incorporating technology as a way of creating an immersive experience for our guests to learn about day-to-day life for people on the streets. This education will be used to not only create more empathy but also for mobilization. When writing what this museum will be about, these words immediately came to me:

> More than one million people are homeless in the United States, a quarter of those being children. Historically, homelessness has been viewed as a character flaw, a personality defect to be looked down on. Many of those experiencing homelessness have not been given an opportunity for another option. Homelessness is systemic, generational, and often times as a result of long-held misconceptions about those experiencing the plight. Their lives are overlooked on street corners, under bridges, and on metal bunk beds in shelters across the country.[4]

The Dignity Museum shares the stories of the forgotten and presents the unjust causes of the disparity in resource allocation. It tells the stories of those who were born into poverty, those who became homeless as adults, the kids holding cardboard signs at the stoplight, and their collective fight to beat their circumstances.

We know how great it is to be seen, heard, acknowledged for who we are, and treated as if we matter. Who doesn't enjoy being recognized for doing a good job or being honored for going beyond the call of duty? We also know what it feels like to be treated as inferior, discriminated against, ignored, misunderstood, criticized, and excluded. There is little worse than being treated unfairly and having no ability to do anything about it, or being excluded from something that means a lot to us. We believe that everyone deserves dignity and everyone's story matters. Therefore, we have vowed to tell the stories of the forgotten as a way of affirming the dignity of all who live on the margins of society.

Thus we chose the name the Dignity Museum. It's unique in that it is housed in a shipping container and has the flexibility to be transported to various places around the city or the country. We hope to partner with like-minded organizations and persons to bring it to unique spaces to educate people on the go. If you know of an organization or school that might be interested in bringing this living museum to their space, feel free to reach out to us.

I hope that we never underestimate the power we have to bring light to dark places by being willing to expose the dark, foreign places within ourselves. I leave you with this verse to ponder.

> If anyone has material possessions and sees a brother or sister in need but has no pity on them, how can the love of God be in that person? Dear children, let us not love with words or speech but with actions and in truth. (1 John 3:17-18)

CHAPTER SIX

YOU ARE PART
OF THE SOLUTION

Before we read about one tragedy, it seems as if another is happening. From police shootings of unarmed black bodies to a homeless man being locked up for three months because the cashier accused him of having a fake ten-dollar bill (which turned out to be real) to gentrification and the poor being displaced—it can overwhelm us and feel like it's impossible for us to contribute anything to solve these ongoing problems in the world.[1]

One question that hangs over our heads when we encounter these stories is, What is my role in this? I discuss this question often with my friend Matt Heath.

We both believe it's easy to look to politicians, nonprofit leaders, and pastors who are working to fight social injustice and underestimate the impact of what a "regular" person might be able to accomplish. We're tempted to underestimate our own influence on such big issues because we either believe the problem is too great or that we are not equipped to make a difference. We often forget how we, as a community, can make a huge difference.

But a dangerous thing happens when we start to believe that story about ourselves, our communities, and the world around us. It's the sort of belief that starts out small—we don't sign up to volunteer, or we drive past someone on the street because we're not sure what to do. Over time, though, it develops into a pattern that tells us we are not part of the solution.

It is difficult to think of yourself as a solution to problems that occur everywhere. However, I am afraid that no one has told you how necessary you are to this world or how valuable what you have to offer is to the big picture of what God is trying to do. Maybe you believe it doesn't matter if you helped, or that real change making belongs to lifelong advocates. That is far from the truth. You have everything you need within you to contribute something meaningful to this world.

I used to believe these sorts of negative assumptions. When I was in high school, I had twenty-five teachers and school staff tell me I wouldn't make it. These teachers had no idea what I was facing in my home life; instead they focused on the negative and even pointed out the worst in me. They didn't see me fully.

My senior year, a classmate and I started arguing and got into a three-minute fight before it was broken up. As we were about to be sent to the principal's office, the substitute teacher pulled me aside and said that even though I was getting in trouble, he thought I was good at public speaking and that I had the potential to be a great leader. His comment changed my life. Who? Me?

Up until then, I had bought into the stories everyone had told me about who I was and what I had to offer. The same lies played over and over in my head: you're not good enough; you're an outcast; you don't belong. It was easier to believe what I heard instead of fighting to become something else. It was my own inner poverty.

I wondered if I was alone in this, if I was the only person to ever let my surroundings dictate who I became. (Spoiler: I wasn't the only one, and neither are you.)

If you're lucky, you'll reach a moment when you realize that the story you've always been told about yourself might not be true, that you're allowed to ask why you've always believed something and then change the next chapter. I don't think God is afraid of our questions. In fact, Jesus was always asking challenging questions in response to the religious leaders.

I'm so glad I questioned the story I had been told most of my life. What if I still believed what my high school teachers had told me about who I was going to become? In fact, I have been back to that school since then and have given lectures to other students and even the faculty.

For most people this sort of shift happens slowly but is instigated by a singular moment—the moment you become open to asking questions about yourself, the world around you, and your role in it. Presently, you're not looking for answers because in most cases there aren't concrete answers to every unique situation. But being open and having a mindset toward growth and betterment and wholeness changes you.

This is what happens when people meet Jesus. Not in the Sunday school kind of way, but rather when they meet God in pain and suffering, in love, and in questions that have no answers. Somehow God is still big enough to hold it all. A drug dealer becomes a small business owner. An insecure mother becomes an author. A young woman in her twenties learns to forgive her parents.

YOU CHOOSE YOUR FUTURE

The journey of changing what we believe is a difficult one. We are comfortable where we are. Most times, what we believe contributes to our entire worldview and what we've built our whole lives on. How could we consider that maybe we've got something wrong about ourselves or the world around us? What if we have something more to offer than we let ourselves believe? What if, in fact, the world really does need what we bring to the table?

The process of realizing what you have to offer and using it in the world consists of two things: first, knowing who God created you to be, and second, recognizing the gifts and talents you have to offer.

The first part of this might sound cliché. What does it mean to know who God created you to be? Do you picture cheesy motivational posters and kids' songs? A lot of this sunk in for me as I read Psalm 139:

> My frame was not hidden from you
> > when I was made in the secret place,
> > when I was woven together in the depths of the earth.
> Your eyes saw my unformed body;
> > all the days ordained for me were written in your book
> > before one of them came to be. (Psalm 139:15-16)

God knew the skills, gifts, talents, failures, and mistakes I would make and loved me anyway. He knew the family I was placed in and everything I would endure in my life. God even created deep meaning from the hardest difficulties and pain I've experienced. I could never serve and work with the people I work with today if I had not known what it feels like to be lost, vulnerable, and unseen. I don't know the answer to why suffering exists, but I do believe a byproduct is that we are connected to one another on a deeper level than we would have been without it. Jesus knows this. When he came to earth, he became connected to us and all humanity in a way we couldn't see before— even in all of the suffering he had to endure.

Second to Jesus, Jacob's son Joseph is my favorite person in the Bible. He's misunderstood, grew up in a dysfunctional family, had a dream, was rejected and sold by his family, and went through thirteen years of trial after trial. He's thrown in jail undeservedly, eventually finds his way out, and is appointed by Pharaoh to rule Egypt during a famine. In Genesis 50 he's confronted by his brothers after years of pain and says, "You intended to harm me, but God intended it for good to accomplish what is now being done, the saving of many lives" (Genesis 50:20).

I'd like to think that most of our stories are like this. Realistically, we're normal people like Joseph was, with messy families, baggage, and hopefully the ability to recognize God in the midst of it. By God's providence, Joseph was shown how valuable his pain and endurance was. I wonder how many people die in the wilderness of never being affirmed or understanding the importance of their pain.

The same was true for Moses, whose mother left him in a basket floating down the river. Rahab was called a harlot but hid and saved Israelites in Jericho. Queen Esther saved the Jewish people from an evil king by speaking up and being brave. These people from the Bible are used by God despite their perceived flaws and imperfections. God can use everyone.

The stories of everyday people who change the landscape and the future aren't only found in the Bible. They're not just ancient stories either. Consider the experiences of Fannie Lou Hamer, Ella Baker, Mamie Till, Bayard Rustin, Daisy Bates, Reverend John Conley, or the many other heroes of the civil rights movement. The same story is true for one of my many inspirations of that era, Dr. Martin Luther King Jr.

Dr. King was an ordinary man born to a pastor and a school-teacher. He grew up in an era when people were treated unfairly and discriminated against based on the color of their skin.

Today Dr. King is a hero. He spent his life fighting for equality and justice among all people. In his own time though, he was hated. The government was against him and his life was threatened constantly.

Dr. King's fight for justice and equality wasn't popular, but he got up every day to do something about it. He started bus boycotts, endured fire hoses and death threats, and sat at lunch tables while people screamed insults at him and told him he was worthless and didn't belong. In his book *April 4, 1968: Martin Luther King Jr.'s Death and How It Changed America*, Michael Eric Dyson reveals that people wanted King dead because they hated him.[2]

King laid the foundation of sacrifice and the example of how God can use us to serve a greater purpose in the world. As he continued fighting for justice, more and more people joined him. So many people joined him and heard him that things began to shift. Slowly, something that had been so common in society was revealed for the evil that it was because someone was brave enough to stand up against it. The movement grew because people started to listen. Ordinary people who believed the injustice was too great to conquer simply started to listen and change what they believed about themselves and the people around them.

It might be difficult to imagine what it might feel like to be told individuals are less valuable or subhuman because of the color of their skin or where they come from. But the poor are told they are less valuable and less human. They have not received the same opportunities as we have, so their families are starving and sleeping under bridges.

The second step in the process of making a difference is recognizing the unique gifts and talents we've each been given.
Like the substitute teacher who helped me realize my gifts
weren't math and science but communicating and bringing
people together, we must recognize the talents we have that are
special to us. Ask, *What am I good at? How do I help others? What
makes me upset?* Many times the things that upset us and create
passion within us are areas where we can make a difference.

Too often I see people on the sidelines admiring others for
certain strengths they have. Don't waste your life wishing you
were someone else. Learn who you are and use your gifts accord-
ingly. It doesn't matter if you're an accountant, writer, artist,
student, cashier, or stay-at-home parent. We all have something
unique and necessary to contribute.

In 1 Corinthians 12, Paul likens the church to a body. The
unique skills of each body part contribute to create a whole,
functioning system. God gives each of us different skills, spiritual gifts, and talents that the world needs. Yours are no mistake.

If you don't know what you're good at, take a personality test,
ask your friends, do something that interests you. Starting to
know yourself now is one of the most important things you can
do in the process of moving forward.

After you know who you are and the talents you have to offer,
you have to learn the people and community needs around you.
I call this proximity. The average person doesn't know what's
happening in the community or often will say something like,
"I don't think our community struggles with poverty." I can
promise you that is not true.

Since 1990, poverty in suburban communities has actually risen
50 percent.[3] It's easy to hide this type of poverty behind closed
doors. In communities with limited opportunities for higher

paying jobs, single-family households struggle financially. Poverty is everywhere. It's important to do your own demographic research to discover what's going on in your own community.

My approach to creative problem solving is similar to design thinking. Design thinking refers to the creative strategies designers use during the process of designing. For me, it gives a systematic approach to go from empathy to the implementation of an idea that can help serve the needs of the people around me. I came up with a modified version of the design-thinking process that helps my personal processes. It's broken down into five words: *discernment, imagine, collaboration, move,* and *impact.*

Discernment. Discernment requires a lot of listening and paying attention to societal and cultural trends. Examine the community around you and get to know the individual people who might be struggling. Listening to the people around you will help point you to the needs of your specific community. Ask what is going on and grow your ability to sift through situations.

Imagine. Imagining involves holding the problem in one hand and thinking about what is at your disposal in the other hand. Ask yourself, *What resources, excess stuff, or opportunities do I have in my own life that could match this need?* This phase is the beginning of the formation of a solution. Imagine you turn a bus into a shower bus or a vacant lot into a tiny village.

Collaboration. I strongly believe that collaboration is one of the greatest keys to solving any major problem. Isolating yourself and coming up with your own singular solutions is never going to create massive change. Once you discern and imagine how to fix a problem, ask, Who do I know who can help? This is the time to use relationships and platforms that already exist to cast a vision and invite people into the journey instead of starting from square one on every issue.

Move. How can you test the solutions formed through collaboration with others? From testing your ideas, you begin to spread your impact. Here the motto is: *impact over perfection.* Don't focus on getting everything right; focus on creating significant change.

The more you do this, the more you will learn about the people around you as you create lasting relationships. The more relationships you create, the more discernment you will also gain. And this will bring you back to the first step so you can repeat the cycle for different needs within the community. This all leads to my favorite part of the process, *impact.*

Impact. At the end of the day, impact is the main goal. You make a difference for those who are in need.

KEEP GOING

When I first turned my life around and started to speak up for the vulnerable and voiceless, my friends and family thought I was just going through a phase. Why would he be doing this? many people asked. I even remember at one point a number of people cut off our friendship because they didn't understand that I was getting my inner worth from another place—my relationship with God. While it hurt that they didn't believe I had really changed, I understood why they thought that. I knew that I had to prove them wrong and even show them that I could rise above the labels and false expectations that people placed one me. I found out early that people don't give me my worth—God does.

I had this image in my mind of the person I used to be on one bridge and the person I now am on another. In my mind I burned the bridge to the person I used to be. I had to visualize that picture and decide I would never be that person again.

I could never go back to those old patterns and selfish behaviors and excuses. I took off the labels of "misfit," "worthless," and "rebel."

To be honest, though, even after I burned the bridge to my former self and removed the labels from my belief system, I still struggled. It wasn't like I waved a magic wand and my troubles disappeared. But in a sense, my old self allowed me to relate to others I encountered and to empower them to become even more than they were before. It gave me a sort of empathy I never could have had without those experiences.

It only worked because every day I got up and just kept going. I moved one step at a time in the direction I wanted, to write my story. I still get nervous in leadership roles and while speaking at public events. I'm very ordinary and passionate, and some days I'm exhausted and take naps. So, if I'm someone who's making a difference—you can too.

A while ago I met this amazing young man named Paul. He came downtown to serve the community with my team. We were setting up for the day and meeting in this big church building. I got up and thanked everyone for coming and quickly spoke a few words on servant leadership. Then I made my way to the back of the auditorium while some of my team members gave instructions for where people were going next.

I saw this young boy get up from his chair in the front and slowly make his way to the back of the auditorium where I was standing. With a big smile on his face he introduced himself and said, "Hey! I'm here to volunteer, but I brought my saxophone and my amps and would really love it if I could play something. Can I play something?"

I was surprised. No one had ever asked me this sort of thing before while we were serving. Honestly, I had no idea if this boy was any good on the saxophone, but I responded, "Sure! Go for it. Set it up."

Paul walked away and grabbed his assistant (who I later found out was his brother) to help him get his equipment from the car. As he brought in his case, amps, and cords, I wondered what I had gotten myself into. I watched them set up and a little bit of a crowd gathered as people got their food and were settling in.

After a few minutes of anticipation, Paul started to play and every head in the building turned. It sounded like something straight off of a jazz CD. The people started dancing and saying, "Ooh, that's my song!" The entire atmosphere of the day shifted. It went from a normal service day to a fun, friendlier, warm environment. Paul brought a depth to the experience that we hadn't realized was missing. By playing music and inviting the people to smile, dance, and laugh together, the event became more than a free handout. The music nourished the people more than a ham sandwich ever could. I wondered if that was a glimpse of what heaven looked like.

This world needs your gifts, and more importantly it needs you. Schedule a time to use your gift, right now, no matter how small you think it might be. We need you to be present, to offer who you are even when you're not sure how it fits. I promise you, if you bring who you are to the table, you are offering more than you can possibly imagine.

CHAPTER SEVEN

DIFFERENT COMMUNITIES, DIFFERENT NEEDS

Last year I traveled to Kentucky to screen a documentary film based on my walk from Atlanta to Washington, DC. It was a campaign called #MAP16 launched to raise awareness about the millions of people in our country suffering from impoverishment. The film shares the stories of the different people I met along the way. It's titled *Voiceless*.[1]

When we arrived in Kentucky, our friend Michael Tucker greeted us at a restaurant that his family owns. In the back of my mind I was nervous that the film wouldn't be received well in a place that did not have much visible poverty. (I found out later, though, that the poverty experienced in this community was very real but different than I first imagined.)

I drove through a small town and passed someone driving a horse and buggy through an Amish community. The women all wore long dresses, and the men had dark suits and suspenders. Driving on the dirt road I wondered, *What would happen if these people with their horse and buggy drove through the streets of Atlanta?*

It's funny to imagine how people might react. I bet there would be a lot of, "What the . . . ?" Honestly, that was my reaction when I first saw the horse and buggy. I had a lot of questions.

This has happened to me a lot throughout the various cultures I've been able to see and experience. Every culture and place has a different way of doing things. These distinctions aren't inherently bad or wrong—just different.

At its most basic, diversity is like having to take your shoes off at a friend's house when you keep your shoes on at your own. Everyone has different rules and ways of life.

After God finished creating the world, he called it good. All of it. I think when he called the different parts good, he was calling the depths of the sea as good as the dry desert. He called the cactus and the rainforest flowers good. He created a diverse world with diverse species and diverse people. I imagine you and I look pretty different, yet we are both good, beautiful beings created by God.

Being different from one another means that we have different ways of learning, different ways of eating, different ways of associating and living, and different sets of problems, concerns, beliefs, and worldviews. When we take that into account, we realize that the way I relate to the world might look different from the way you relate to the world. That often means that what I think you might need to solve a certain problem looks different from what you might actually need.

When I got my degree in counseling, one of the classes I had to take was cultural diversity. This class helped me understand the unique approach to counseling people from different backgrounds. There are different cultural behaviors, worldviews, and value systems that make each counseling relationship unique. Cultural diversity also refers to having different cultures respect each other's differences.

I run into this a lot as my dream is to eradicate systemic poverty. A lot of people think they know the answers. With good reason—we're trained to evaluate problems, look at the symptoms, and figure out what the cure is. Sometimes, though, we miss the beautiful diversity we've been created with, not realizing that rarely is there a one-size-fits-all, standard cure for the poor. We've seen this flesh out in the media in different ways when people make blanket statements without fully understanding another person's world.

I have had this happen to me as an African American when my friends of another race suggest that policing issues aren't bad in our country. But they don't have to wake up in fear of police officers because of the color of their skin.

IMAGINE THIS WITH ME

Imagine the following scenario. You wake up one morning with a stuffy nose and a sore throat. You remember hearing that someone at the office had the flu, so you decide to be careful. If you're not feeling better in a day you tell yourself you'll go to the clinic downtown. The next morning you wake up exhausted, your head pounding, achy knees, and your throat and nose are even worse. You drive straight to the doctor's office and check in with the nurse at the front desk.

The nurse asks you what your symptoms are and asks you to take a seat in the waiting room. Fifteen minutes later the nurse calls your name, hands you a small slip of paper, and says, "Thanks for coming in! Have a nice day." Confused, you look at the paper and see it's a prescription for an allergy medication.

"Excuse me," you say to the nurse, "but I think I might have the flu. You must have given me the wrong slip. I haven't even been in to see the doctor yet."

"Oh, no," the nurse replies, "that's the right slip. I told the doctor your symptoms, and he said the pollen count went up last week and your symptoms are clear. You just need some extra-strength allergy pills to get you through. The doctor knows what he's talking about."

A little frustrated and desperate you tell the nurse, "I'm sorry, but you don't understand. Someone in my office had the flu this week, and I've never had allergies before."

"That's the doctor's diagnosis. That's all I can do for you. Thanks for coming in. Have a nice day, and I hope your allergies clear up soon."

Maybe this sounds extreme or like something that would never happen. But this is what we're doing every day when we prescribe answers for the problems of people we've never seen or met.

One of my favorite things about Jesus is how much he saw people. In the Gospels there are dozens of verses that say, "Jesus saw." Here's why I find that phrase so interesting. It's often used when setting up a story, like when Jesus saw the man at the pool of Bethesda (John 5:6) or when he saw a woman who had been crippled for eighteen years (Luke 13:12).

I've always imagined that this type of "seeing" isn't the kind of seeing we do when we drive by someone at a stoplight. It's the kind of seeing that happens when we're sitting across from a friend at a coffee shop. It requires more than a quick glance. I think Jesus was looking into someone's soul, reading between the lines, and seeing them for everything they were. Only then did he heal sight, restore the lame, and cast out demons.

The type of seeing Jesus did became the door to proximity where he could engage and talk to the person in front of him. He responded to the information given to him by the person in front of him. Whether the individual was blind or his daughter had died, Jesus saw people first, then he engaged, then he responded. He saw these people in their full humanity, with dignity, and with an openness to meet them where they were. We first have to learn to see.

I'll never forget encountering a story that broke my heart. I love to work out of coffee shops. There's something about being in an environment where people are busy, making connections, and in many instances making things happen. However, there is also risk in sitting in coffee shops in urban centers being gentrified.

Many days when working in coffee shops I see people experiencing homelessness, hoping someone will buy them a cup of coffee. Every now and then someone wins the "charity" lottery and is given a cup. But this lottery doesn't come without having to endure cold stares, mean mugs, and vile statements.

One day recently I was sitting in a coffee shop when I noticed an African American man standing outside and heard a group of young, white adults talking about him a few tables over from me. The African American man, whose name I don't know, wore socks that were a dingy brown and a pair of jeans that hadn't been washed in weeks or months. The jeans had a hole the size of a basketball in one of the legs, and it was obvious the man wasn't wearing undergarments.

The men wearing suits and drinking hot coffee began to laugh at the man outside. They were louder than I expected them to be, and they didn't seem to mind that anyone could overhear their slurs and jokes toward the man outside.

The homeless man, who seemed to gather up enough change to buy a cup of coffee, walked inside, and one of the young men turned to him and said, "Why don't you get a job and stop begging people for money?"

Another chimed in and said, "He can't get a job looking like a throwaway."

The third man added something that pierced me too, "Why are they so lazy? Geez."

As I was about to stand up and defend the man, a coffee shop employee came over to the men and asked them to leave. This is a true story. These young men represented what happens when we don't embrace diversity.

BE AWARE, BE CAREFUL

Recently, I was talking to one of my friends who does work in an urban community and asked him how the work was going. He said, "Well, we actually had some of the people we were serving say that they hated it when the 'church folks' came to help. I went down to ask the people what happened to figure out why they felt that way."

My friend asked them, "Hey, I heard you guys weren't super happy some of the people from the church were coming around. Why is that? Don't you want your lawn mowed or your house painted?"

"Sure," the man told my friend, "but they say mean things, and I don't want to get hurt."

"What do you mean? What would they say?" my friend asked.

"Well, yeah they paint the house, but when they come over they make statements like, 'Oh wow, your children are so well behaved' and 'Wow, you keep your house clean.' I don't like that. Just because I have less doesn't mean I don't have morals or ethics to care for the things I have."

I'm sure the people painting the house meant no harm with what they said. But it showed the person in poverty that the person who came to paint his house must have believed that material possessions (or lack thereof) dictate the kind of person he is. This is where helping can hurt and why doctors must see patients before prescribing medication.

When we think that someone needs house painting more than to be empowered, something is wrong.

It's important to know the difference between what strips dignity from people and what affirms the dignity of people. The following lists will help us to know the difference.

AFFIRMING DIGNITY

Noticing people and valuing people the way Jesus does. Jesus made it his priority to express that he highly valued those he stopped to communicate with. No matter who they were, he saw the best in them.

Giving options to people. Just because people are without doesn't mean they can't make decisions and have preferences. Earlier I mentioned a volunteer who got mad at a person we were helping because he chose something different. We must allow people the option of choice.

Listening to those who are vulnerable. Something magical happens when we stop and pause long enough to listen to people. You know how it feels to be listened to about what you've faced lately. The same is true for those we notice and see.

Empowering people. Empowering someone can be as simple as sharing wisdom with and teaching someone. I personally would not be where I am without people being willing to share their knowledge with me.

THINGS THAT CAN REMOVE DIGNITY

Forcing change. We should never try to force people to change. God is patient with us, so we should be patient with others.

Using stereotypical language that is both abusive and offensive.
We must be careful how we talk to those we seek to help. If we
aren't careful, our words can do more harm than good.

Excluding people or including them with limitations. We should aim
to be more inclusive instead of excluding others because of
their poverty.

*Solving problems with money rather giving ourselves to solve the
problems with talents and gifts.* We must watch out for trying
to solve problems with money alone instead of giving people
the one thing they need most—relationships.

THE WHEEL OF WELLNESS

My office is in College Park in Atlanta, and there is a lack of
grocery stores that give people access to healthy foods.

In Flint, Michigan (and other countries around the world),
there is a lack of clean public drinking water and a high unemployment rate due to the nearby factories that have shut down.

Flint and College Park are two different communities that
struggle with different problems contributing to and propelling
systemic poverty. The most useful tool I've used to identify these
different types of needs within a community is called the Wheel
of Wellness.

The original Wheel of Wellness model was based on individual psychology by Thomas J. Sweeney and Melvin Witmer.
Later, it was modified by Jane E. Myers. Surrounding the individual in the Wheel of Wellness are life forces that affect
personal wellness: family, religion, education, business/industry,
media, government, and community. Global forces are also de-
picted as affecting the individual.[2]

Today people use variations of the original Wheel of Wellness
to understand what it takes to bring their areas of focus to a
place of wellness. The Wheel of Wellness I use is simpler and

focuses on these areas: physical, emotional, occupational, spiritual, environmental, social, intellectual, and financial.[3] Each of these words on a basic level gives us a glimpse of eight areas that help a person to be holistically well. Most often, we cling to the physical needs that we can meet for someone. It's easier, simpler, and much more comfortable to paint someone's house and bring them groceries than to help them figure out an emotional, intellectual, or social need.

Meeting a physical need is important. It can often be the first step in helping someone. These needs are at the bottom of Maslow's hierarchy of needs, the basic things a human needs to survive. What can happen, though, is that we help people survive but don't invest in what it takes to bring someone to holistic wellness. These other pieces of wellness move people from survival to escaping the systemic type of poverty that keeps families trapped for generations.

Living in a food desert without access to healthy foods will affect the physical part of a person's wellness, while living in a community with a high unemployment rate will have a greater impact on someone's financial and occupational wellness. In a community with a high rate of single moms, we might see that they're struggling socially, but in a community with a poor education system, those people might be struggling intellectually.

These different needs can only be discerned by entering into a community and listening to the stories of the people who live there. If we hear the cries and discern the needs through those conversations, we can then use the wheel to understand their needs better and also see what solutions can be implemented to make the greatest impact on the needs that directly affect that specific community.

Once we identify some of these needs, we are able to more directly design what I call problem-solving solutions to address them. What could we do to address the physical issue? Could we start a walking group? Could we build a gym? Could we retrofit something? What can we organize people around?

If there's a spiritual lack, how could we partner with churches in the community to be a funnel into spaces that allow people to connect with the divine?

If the issue is intellectual, how can we introduce and bring people into new ideas and opportunities rather than the ones that have surrounded them their entire lives?

The Wheel of Wellness first gives the tools to go into a community and see what might be lacking or missing in these people's journey toward wellness. It then provides a framework to create innovative solutions to meet their needs. Each community is diverse, different, and needs unique attention.

MENTAL HEALTH

As we talk about these specific needs, I want to briefly, purposefully, take a moment to touch on mental health, which is a huge piece of the Wellness Wheel and a barrier for so many on their journey toward wholeness. Mental health is a complicated and vast issue that sometimes has no answers. Mental health refers to our psychological and emotional well-being. If a person's overall mental health is lacking, mental illness sometimes comes into the picture. Interestingly enough, mental illness doesn't discriminate.

Someone you know—or maybe even you—has probably dealt with some mental health challenges. The difference between the people you know and the ones who are in poverty or are homeless because of their challenges is almost always a network of people and the ability to pay for proper health care.

If you are experiencing anxiety, I imagine you have a few people in your contact list who you could call. And if not, most likely you have health care that allows you the opportunity to talk to a counselor.

What does it look like to experience anxiety, depression, or another mental illness and not have a social network, a church, or a family that can help? What if you experience these things without a job that has health care benefits? Mental illness is hard to overcome no matter who you are, but it's decidedly harder without help.

We people in the church have to get real about mental health. I could list pages of resources, but we need to be honest, open up, and provide safe places to talk about mental health. We fear talking about mental health and engaging in conversations with people who have mental health issues. It's uncomfortable to care for someone we might perceive to be unbalanced, but mental health problems are more common than we imagine among the people sitting in our churches and in our own families, just as it is in communities experiencing poverty.

Here are a few resources we should be aware of in relating to mental health as a community of faith:

SITES

aacc.net
counseling.org
hope4mentalhealth.com
mentalhealthgracealliance.org
apa.org

BOOKS

Darkness Is My Only Companion: A Christian Response to Mental Illness by Kathryn Greene-McCreight

Grace for the Afflicted: A Clinical and Biblical Perspective on Mental Illness
   by Matthew S. Stanford
Moving from Shame to Self-Worth by Edward P. Wimberly
Using Scripture in Pastoral Counseling by Edward P. Wimberly
Churches That Heal: Becoming a Church That Mends Broken Hearts and Restores Shattered Lives by Doug Murren
Bipolar Faith: A Black Woman's Journey with Depression and Faith by Monica A. Coleman
Troubled Minds: Mental Health and the Church's Mission by Amy Simpson

VIDEOS

Creating Caring Congregations by Mental Health Ministries, California-Pacific Annual Conference of the United Methodist Church
Of Two Minds, directed by Douglas Blush and Lisa J. Klein
The Soloist, directed by Joe Wright
A Beautiful Mind, directed by Ron Howard
Frankie & Alice, directed by Geoffrey Sax
Same Kind of Different as Me, directed by Michael Carney

ORGANIZATIONS

American Psychological Association
Anabaptist Disabilities Network
Center for Spirituality, Theology and Health
Depression and Bipolar Support Alliance
Health Ministries Association
Lift Disability Network
Lutheran Network for Mental Illness/Brain Disorders
Mental Health America
Mental Health Ministries
Mental Illness Network of the United Church of Christ
National Alliance on Mental Illness
NAMI FaithNet
National Association of Catholic Chaplains
National Institute of Mental Health

Pathways to Promise

QPR Institute—Suicide Prevention Training

SAVE: Suicide Awareness Voices of Education

Suicide Prevention Resource Center

While I was working on my counseling degree, I learned this secret: *ask questions and listen.* You don't need all the answers; you actually don't need any answers. It's as simple as entering into the world of others without having answers but simply responding and being present. If they need more help, help them find it.

GOOD QUESTIONS

A few weeks ago a family showed up to our office for our "Love Feeds" program, where we distribute groceries to families in the community. The couple walked through the door with their child, and I noticed right away that they were sweating a lot more than the other people who had been coming to the office that day. Normally I don't notice or make comments on anyone's physical appearance when they arrive at our center, but I could tell something was different for this family. Even their two-year-old was sweating. They introduced themselves as Chris and Ashley.

After a few minutes of conversation, I found out that this family had walked five miles just for diapers and the baby was eating spaghetti sauce instead of baby food. I asked them a little more about what was going on. They said they were in their twenties, and I asked if they had any family members that could help them. Both of their parental figures had died while they were in their teens, so they had assumed adult responsibilities early on in their lives. They had virtually raised themselves.

Over time, my team was able to walk alongside Chris and Ashley, teach them to drive, help them get their driver's licenses, and even bless them with a donated car.

Helping this family wasn't just giving them the two bags of groceries that we give out in our program. But helping them also wasn't as complicated as coming up with a fourteen-step plan. It started by asking a couple of questions. We use questions like these in order to find out why someone's world is the way it is.

- What's your name?
- How long have you lived here?
- Does your family live around here?
- Do you have a community that supports you?

Conversation creates the bridge for friendship and community. These things that seem small and simple are the foundational pieces for beginning to cure our own spiritual poverty. We use these pieces to connect and find home and spiritual community with one another.

THEIR STORIES AND YOUR STORY

As I asked more questions of Chris and Ashley, layer after layer of their story peeled back. I heard and felt the pain they experienced from not having a mother figure in their lives. They shared how no one had ever taught them to drive, which brought me back to myself at sixteen sitting in the car with different people who took the time to teach me how to drive.

The more I heard their story, the stronger I felt their lack. I saw how limited they were in what they were able to do and accomplish. I wondered what they would be able to pass on to their kids. This family was just one example of so many people whose stories go unheard and whose needs are unmet.

Their story broke me and revealed to me parts of my own story that connected with theirs and other parts I was grateful for. Our stories are all more intertwined than we think. As you approach this work and listen to the stories of others, if you are open you will hear and learn things about yourself that you might have not known before.

It reminds me of Paul's writing in 2 Corinthians 5:17, "Therefore, if anyone is in Christ, he is a new creation. The old has passed away; behold, the new has come" (ESV).

In my own spiritual poverty, Christ stepped in for me, and my life never looked the same. In the same fashion, how can we do for others what Christ has done for us? How can we see people where they are, just as Jesus did for us, and offer them more than a painted house or a bag of groceries?

CHAPTER EIGHT

DIGNITY AND HOW TO SEE PEOPLE

A few months back I was walking through downtown Chicago with my wife. As in every city, people experiencing homelessness were sitting on the sidewalks, asking for change. One man asked me if I could buy him some food. Anytime someone asks me that specific question, I stop. If we're near a restaurant, I'll go into the place and buy the person a meal. I asked him his name; surprised, he said Julius.

We had just passed a fried-chicken restaurant, so I said, "Come on, let's go in here." I opened the door for him so he could walk in first. As soon as he and I entered, every head in the place turned and looked at us, more specifically, at him. The stares of the people behind the counter were obvious. They looked at one another and then back at him with furrowed brows—looks that made us both uncomfortable.

We approached the counter to order, and I told the woman behind the register, "I've got whatever he wants." Then I turned to him and asked, "So, what do you want?"

Julius picked out some chicken, and I asked him, "You sure that's all you want?" And he ordered a couple other pieces.

The disapproving looks and whispers continued. The woman behind the counter continued to talk to me even though I wasn't ordering. They were sending a clear message to Julius: *you* don't belong here. There's no space for you here. You're not valued here.

We don't want you here. In this case, the "here" where Julius didn't belong was in a fast-food restaurant.

It's hard for me to not get angry in situations like these. I want to buy all the chicken in the restaurant and invite in every person on the streets. Maybe one day I'll do that. I'm confused and hurt that we think we have the power to strip someone of the value and right to be in a space. We're trying to take their dignity.

This happens all over the country and around the world. It happens to people who are experiencing homelessness as they try to get water or use the restroom in a restaurant. It happens in other countries when laws prohibit women from driving and going to school. It happens in cities that prohibit giving out food or distributing health care. It happens when children are taken away from refugee mothers at our country's border. We strip people of their dignity and worth. This is antithetical to *seeing* people and affirming their dignity.

It also happens on a personal level when we judge or are biased toward people not like us. It reminds me of how judgmental the Pharisees were toward people who did not fit into their religious boxes. We damage people when we judge them, dismiss them, and act mean toward them because they are not like us. When Jesus told us to "love your neighbor," he was actually commanding us to love people who are not like us.

Why? Because it's easy to love people you know. It's a lot tougher to love people you don't know.

If Jesus would have personally turned people away, we would have a different picture of our Savior. Jesus is asking us to do what makes us uncomfortable: loving people who need it the most— even if we are not like them.

Jesus almost always affirmed people who would have been denounced or rejected by the religious leaders of his day. He affirmed a woman who was seen as missing the mark of God, ate with tax collectors, healed and comforted a woman who had an issue of blood, spoke to a man possessed by a demon, and drank water from the woman at the well. These are people who would have not been *seen* during the days Jesus walked the earth.

The New Testament includes many examples of Jesus showing love to people who would have been dismissed. Using Jesus' example, we have a model of how to share the love of God with outcasts.

WELCOMING PEOPLE

A coffee shop in Atlanta has modeled what it means to see and welcome people. One day, I was sitting outside this coffee shop and a husband and wife who were experiencing homelessness walked toward the coffee shop. As they started to enter, I hoped this coffee shop wouldn't turn them away.

However, something was different with this company, and to my surprise, the workers were friendly and even gave this couple coffee. This blew my mind. I later found out that this store does this all the time as a way of embracing people struggling with this plight.

I also read an article about a pizza shop in New York that gives a slice of pizza away to people experiencing homelessness each time a regular customer buys a slice of pizza. Anytime I experience or hear stories like these, it does my heart good. I wonder what type of difference we could all make if we, like Jesus, saw people and welcomed them like these coffee shops and pizza parlors. I bet that would affirm the dignity of those who feel cast aside in our society.

WHAT IS DIGNITY?

What is dignity? And where does it come from? At its simplest, dignity is the quality of being worthy of honor and respect. I believe that dignity is the inherent worth and value of a person. But what makes something worthy?

We assign worth to small trinkets or heirlooms from our childhood, a sentimental value we measure by how much something means to us. We also assign monetary value to just about every other material thing. What makes one car more expensive than the other? Is it always the quality and engineering inside, or is it also the prestige of a BMW over a Toyota?

Value and worth can be attached to material objects, but when it comes to measuring the immaterial, dignity alone applies. I've found we blur the lines between the two—hence the scene in the fried-chicken shop. We are tempted to misplace and measure dignity by net worth, appearance, and material possessions.

Two things need to change: first, the way we, as individuals, treat these people as we're passing by, and second, how we as a community work together to solve these issues from a systemic standpoint. What needs to happen in a culture for this sort of shift to occur? How do we do something as complicated as proving our worth to one another?

Asking these questions reminds me of Genesis—the creation of all things, including you, me, and the man on the street corner. Genesis 1:27 says,

> So God created mankind in his own image,
>> in the image of God he created them;
>> male and female he created them.

It should be as simple as that. As men and women designed in the image of the intelligent designer, we have worth and value.

However, most societies haven't always held these ideals as true. Some effects still linger today.

THE WALK TO MEMPHIS

On March 3, 2018, I began my second March Against Poverty. I would walk from the Center for Civil and Human Rights in downtown Atlanta to the Lorraine Motel in Memphis, Tennessee. The walk was over four hundred miles, and I was set to arrive on April 4, the fiftieth anniversary of the assassination of Dr. Martin Luther King Jr. at the Lorraine Motel. To get from Atlanta to Memphis, I'd have to walk through rural parts of Georgia, Alabama, Mississippi, and Tennessee. Maybe that last sentence doesn't mean much to you. If it doesn't—you most likely don't look like me. If you don't know me, you should know that I'm an African American man. That means that in many cases I'd be walking through small communities of people who have historically and presently expressed bias against people of color.

One day I was walking through a small town in Alabama right after crossing the Georgia state line. The Confederate flag count was rising, which made me cautious of my surroundings— not out of disrespect for the flag but because what the Confederate flag represents to African American people, just as the Nazi flag is a sign of slaughter and murder for Jews. The Confederate flag represents oppression and slavery for African Americans. It makes an African American like me think about the Jim Crow laws that were used to abuse many blacks in the United States.

I was halfway through the walk and my feet were tired and aching, so I started using a walking stick to support myself. I had been walking for an hour or two that morning when over the stretch of road in front of me I saw flashing red and blue lights—the police. They reached me and the two people walking with me and jumped out of their car with their hands on their guns.

They looked at me and shouted, "We got some calls that you've been walking up and down the highway disturbing the community."

I was shaking as they got closer. This sort of interaction is the one I'd feared. I wondered if there'd be headlines, "Black Man Shot on Side of Road by Police." Maybe that seems far-fetched, but at that moment I knew my response to these police officers could be that serious.

Slowly, I pulled out the documents that supported my story of marching for the poor. I had news articles, press releases, and whatever documents I could find to prove that I wasn't to be feared and that my presence as a black man walking down the side of the road was justified. I could not tell him, "I am a parent, a man of faith, a fighter for good, a nonviolent man." All I could do to prove my belonging there was to show him my papers.

A few days later, I was walking, past a high school when a big, red truck with red clay on the tires and a Confederate flag sticker on the bumper passed me multiple times. The truck finally pulled up next to me as I was walking, and a man wearing a white tank top leaned out the window. He locked eyes with me and continued his stare as he roared his engine. I'll never forget those eyes. It was an intense stare like the ones my friend received in the fried-chicken shop in Chicago, like I was in a place where I did not belong.

To confirm my suspicions, the man yelled at me, "You better be safe around here, boy. You don't know where you are." Chills

ran through my body as he sped off, leaving me and my friend
Trey staring at each other in the dust of his tires.

In moments like these I'm confronted with the stark reality
that some people might not like me because of the color of my
skin. The concept is dehumanizing, discouraging, and extremely
difficult to wrestle with. I often find myself asking why, to process
these kinds of situations. These occurrences happened so fre-
quently during my walk to Memphis that a white friend actually
took an entire month off work to walk with me for my safety.

So why did I need to prove my belonging to the police officer?
And why did he believe I needed to prove myself? Why did the
man in the truck tell me to be safe? Why was I so unwelcome
to occupy a small piece of sidewalk on a dirty, rural highway?

Of course, there are a hundred different factors—some I can
never account for. These people's backgrounds, what they were
taught growing up, the news stories they've heard, the hidden
bias and messaging within their community—the reasons are
endless. Regardless of what was behind it, their judgment of
who I am and how they needed to treat me was made long
before they saw me or heard my name. That is what it looks like
to strip a human of dignity.

Throughout my fight for the poor, and especially after these
moments, I think back to the civil rights era, when people who
look like me were fighting for basic human rights and for their
dignity to be recognized by all. Ringing in my mind was a
statement by Dr. King: "Darkness cannot drive out darkness;
only light can do that. Hate cannot drive out hate; only love can
do that."[1]

So I kept walking, even though my questions about why these
people treated me as though I couldn't belong in that space and
why I had no dignity there remained unanswered.

Those moments of not belonging in a chicken shop and on the highway are powerful events. What is worse, though, is what happens over time as a person's identity is slowly eaten away.

LABELS AND AFTERMATH

How do you know where your favorite soda is when you're at the grocery store? Or your favorite candy bar? It's because the label on the can or the packaging tells you what's inside. Labels can have a similar effect on people. They're powerful. What you tell people about who they are has a significant impact on who they become.

Can you imagine day after day walking into a grocery store and being told, "Hey, you don't belong here"? Just as you're being told that, other customers walk past you without anything being said to them. How would that make you feel? Probably frustrated at first. But I imagine the more someone told you that you didn't belong, the more likely you'd eventually believe it.

It's easy to internalize how you've been treated, and eventually that belief will be expressed through your behavior. It becomes a self-fulfilling prophecy, but one that you have been taught to believe about yourself. I can personally relate. I have been labeled many things in life that I had to overcome.

The man experiencing homelessness who was told he didn't belong in the chicken shop must struggle to figure out what it means to belong in a space and battle to believe that he belongs.

When I was treated differently because of the color of my skin, I had to fight a lot of these labels too. On the side of the highway, I felt isolated, alone, depressed, hopeless, and at times like I just wanted to go home to be someplace I was welcome. It's easy to forget you belong. And this applies to more than just homeless men in chicken shops and black men on highways. It also applies to you.

Research shows that what people believe about themselves determines a lot of what they will accomplish or what they will allow themselves to achieve. Susan Biali writes, "There are all these wonderful, capable people walking around out there who believe ridiculous things about themselves that someone else planted in their heads and hearts. They've believed these lies for so long that they don't question them and often never have. The lies inevitably cripple them in some way, often significantly."[2] It's horrible when we are the people behind the perpetuation of these beliefs in others.

Have you ever felt like you didn't belong somewhere? Maybe you're the skinny guy at the gym or the woman on the board of directors. Or you're at a table where everyone is talking about how wonderfully their family is doing and you're afraid to be honest about the hardship your family is going through for fear of what they'll think about you. Over time, if we let these beliefs about ourselves consume us, we'll stop showing up to these places and convince ourselves that we don't belong.

That is where we lose a part of who we are. And if we're not careful, we'll do it to the people around us by telling them who they are and where they belong. People don't become what you want them to become, they become what you encourage them to become.

So if we have all this power, what will we choose to do with it? How will we affirm dignity within others?

RECOGNIZING DIGNITY

I met a man named Charles as he was cutting the grass of a neighbor's yard. He was living on the streets behind a nearby church. We became friends, and I learned that he was extremely talented at creating things with his hands. I started to connect him with people who could teach him more about woodworking and craftsmanship. He began creating art and furniture from old wood pallets he rescued from dumpsters.

The more he created, the more he was able to work, earn a living, and do something that he loved. After a few months, we threw an art show that featured people who struggled with poverty but also loved to create. Hundreds of people came to the show to support the artists. I got up on stage and introduced Charles as one of the main artists. He walked on stage, beaming, proud of his art and accomplishments. I gave him the microphone and he shared about the process behind the art, why he made what he made, and why he chose the different phrases that were on some of the pieces. He was not only invited into the space but was also given a voice, and it started by asking questions and listening to his story.

That night hundreds of people affirmed his dignity. It's not always hundreds of people. Most times it's just a single person who says, "I see you. I'm listening. You belong in this space." Isn't that what we're all longing to hear?

Jesus treated people like this. He spoke to the woman at the well when interacting with such people was looked down on. He didn't laugh at the boy who brought him a few fish and loaves to feed thousands. When the soldier who was arresting Jesus got his ear cut off, Jesus still healed him. Jesus even listened to the thief on the cross and told him, "You will be with me."

As Christians, we believe that all are born with dignity, fashioned carefully and with love by the Creator. Therefore we are commanded to treat everyone fairly and with love.

James 2 says,

My brothers and sisters, believers in our glorious Lord Jesus Christ must not show favoritism. Suppose a man comes into your meeting wearing a gold ring and fine clothes, and a poor man in filthy old clothes also comes in. If you show special attention to the man wearing fine clothes and say, "Here's a good seat for you," but say to the poor man, "You stand there" or "Sit on the floor by my feet," have you not discriminated among yourselves and become judges with evil thoughts?

Listen, my dear brothers and sisters: Has not God chosen those who are poor in the eyes of the world to be rich in faith and to inherit the kingdom he promised those who love him? But you have dishonored the poor. Is it not the rich who are exploiting you? Are they not the ones who are dragging you into court? Are they not the ones who are blaspheming the noble name of him to whom you belong?

If you really keep the royal law found in Scripture, "Love your neighbor as yourself," you are doing right (James 2:1-8).

CONFRONTING OUR BELIEFS

How can we change our default setting to see equal dignity in each person we pass, whether it's the homeless man sitting outside in the rain or the woman ordering coffee in line in front of you?

First, we must check our thoughts and become aware of them. Why should we check our thoughts about the people near us? Because some of our thoughts have been fashioned from being around people who have displayed actions that we thought were unacceptable. There's a difference between living out of habit and living out of intent. There's a difference between living out of what we know is the right thing to do and the sin that keeps us from missing the mark of God. It's the thoughts we have in the moments we're around others different from us that we need to challenge.

We must identify our learned prejudice and sin, then dare to take steps away from it, especially if this is deep in our hearts.

Second, we must ask why seven times. Asking why seven times is one of the greatest ways I have found to get at the root of a thought or idea. (It also dismantles the stereotypes we believe, if we are able to answer with an open heart and with no prejudices.) For example:

I think that the homeless man is lazy and doesn't want to work.

Why do you think that?

Well, because he doesn't have a job.

Why doesn't he have a job?

Most likely he has no ID to get a job.

Why doesn't he have an ID?

His ID was stolen with his bag.

Why was it stolen?

He was in a shelter where everyone was in survival mode, so they stole his stuff.

Why is everyone in survival mode?

They're in survival mode because they haven't eaten or slept in days.

Why haven't the eaten or slept?

They have no one to call for help.

Why?

They do not have the same support system or opportunities I have been given.

The seven whys help us challenge the first negative view of a situation, transforming it into a more understanding and positive thought.

Third, we must replace the negative thought with the full picture and deconstructed view of what might really be going on. What if we took the same list and replaced our initial responses with some that would put us in a place of service instead of a place of judgment and condemnation?

DIGNITY IS SIMPLE

A basketball coach in his early thirties brought his entire team to our center to serve the local community. People formed a line as they waited to get different types of resources. One man who was waiting in line wasn't wearing a shirt. Waiting in line to receive food and clothes is not for the proud; for many it can feel like a difficult or shameful place.

The coach saw the man without a shirt and told one of his players to run to the van and grab an extra shirt. The kid ran to the car and the coach took off his shirt and placed it on the homeless man.

We were sitting with that homeless man a while later and he said, "Man, I really appreciate this." He started to tear up and continued, "Last night I got jumped, and they took my clothes and ripped my shirt off."

The students with the coach didn't walk away with an exact formula or the ABCs of showing someone dignity, but they walked away with the idea that affirming someone's dignity can happen anywhere at any time. You only need to make yourself available.

Sometimes there's not a set of rules for showing others dignity. It's an instinctive desire to make the world a better place even if that looks like taking off your shirt and giving it to someone who doesn't have one. It's knowing that despite the internal poverty that we may have, God still deems us worthy enough to give us the ultimate gift of Jesus.

Dignity is powerful. That many people have lost their lives without knowing they were worthy and valuable scares me. There are so many people who have yet to hear the words, "I love you," and "You matter."

As people who desire to emulate Jesus, we can't go another day without telling the unseen, unheard, and not-valued people that they are loved, seen, and valued.

CHAPTER NINE

CREATING COMMUNITIES

I love movies. They've always been an escape for me. The way they tell stories and bring me on a journey is something that always inspires me. I saw a movie on Netflix called *Imperial Dreams*. The story follows a young African American teen just released from prison who is determined to live a life different from the one that landed him in prison. He's reunited with his son and family in Los Angeles, but back in the same environment it's difficult to become someone else.

The story has stuck with me. The young man in the movie fights desperately for a different way of life—to the point of sleeping in his car to avoid getting involved in the gang his family is in. He struggles to find a job as an ex-convict and is told he can't get his license back until he pays child support. But he can't get a job without a valid ID. The system makes it difficult for him to have the opportunities we all take for granted.

This story makes me wonder what it would look like if this same young man was dropped into a privileged community. What would be different if he knew someone who could help him get a job? Or if he had a mentor who looked like him and had succeeded in creating a new life for himself? He barely knew it was possible to choose a life other than the one he had grown up in. There was no way for this young man to connect with a safe place or group of people who desired a better life for him.

This could have been me. I was involved in gang activity as a young African American man and made one mistake that landed me in jail. Luckily, the charges were dropped because my mother begged the owner of the store I had broken into. It isn't hard to imagine what would have happened if I had gone to prison. My life would look very different now.

The night I spent in jail I met a middle-aged man in the holding cell who looked at me and said, "Why are you wasting your life? Get out of here and do something with your life. Go back to church." So I prayed one of those desperate prayers, "God, if you get the charges dropped, I promise I'll change the way I'm living." Now I'm not saying those sorts of prayers always work, but I also think that prayer in a desperate time has a special place in God's heart.

After the charges were dropped, I made the decision to change the trajectory of my life. I stopped partying and hanging out with the group of friends I was acquainted with. I even physically changed where I was living to give myself a fresh start. I went back to church and surrounded myself with people who took me into their family and helped me create a new version of myself—the home that I was searching for was found in this community. It was a huge shift in my life, and I believe it wouldn't have been possible without a strong community around me.

The shift in my own life led me to believe that it's not possible to create a major lifestyle change without community. God created us to be in community with one another, and we can't live as we are meant to live alone.

FINDING COMMUNITY

We have existed in tribes and communities since the beginning of the world. From the Tower of Babel in Genesis, where all people were separated by their languages, to the divided world we live in today, God created us to be and exist in communities, not in isolation.

I've found that there are three different ways to exist in a community: we can be born into it, we can find it, or we can create it.

Community of our birth. As an African American man, I've had the opportunity to be a part of a beautiful, inspiring, uplifting community. When one of us succeeds, we all succeed. We are tied together as a people who have overcome many obstacles and much opposition. This is the community I was born into, and I am proud to be a part of it.

Throughout my childhood, I remember my grandfather Carlton York sharing what it was like going to a segregated school and having to drink from a water fountain labeled "colored." This community shaped me. I am who I am because of these parts of my story.

In a *Smithsonian* article on racial segregation and American cities, Katie Nodjimbadem observes,

> In *The Color of Law: A Forgotten History of How Our Government Segregated America*, Richard Rothstein, a research associate at the Economic Policy Institute, aims to flip the assumption that the state of racial organization in American cities is simply a result of individual prejudices. He untangles a century's worth of policies that built the segregated American city of today.[1]

Right after the Great Depression, a practice called *redlining* was introduced that divided America cities into different groups based on community demographics. This systematically denied services to residents of specific areas. Most often these areas were defined by race. Banks used these maps to deny home loans to African Americans, and some companies even used the system to deny insurance or health care. Redlining discriminated against minorities, and the negative effects haunt these communities today. The Federal Reserve Bank of Chicago analyzed the data from "redline maps" and found that fifty years later racial segregation, homeownership, home values, and credit scores still show the effects of redlining. While researchers can't say that these maps alone created this inequality, the self-fulfilling prophecies are evident.

Redlining still affects the community I was born into.

But our neighborhood or city isn't the only community we were born into. Many of us were born into dysfunctional or fractured families. We might have been born into privilege or destitution, into communities that were diverse or homogeneous. We are born with religious backgrounds and belief systems in place, whether we agree with them or not as we get older.

Sociologist George Herbert Mead believed that the mind and self are developed as a result of a social process.[2] He argued that how people come to view themselves is based to a large extent on their interactions with others.

Naturally, we must ask next, What effect does the community I was born into have on my life? What does that mean for what I want for my future?

Community we find. Besides the community we are born into, there is the community that we find. In high school and college, I found my community in parties and gang-related friends. In my early twenties when I shifted direction and decided to go back to finish college, more of my community was found in church. My transition back into the church wasn't necessarily what you might think. I didn't go from baggy clothes and smoking weed one week to a holy, suit-and-tie Christian the next week.

One Sunday I was sitting in the back row of church just after I had moved back to Atlanta after getting into some trouble. Skeptical of the church but desperate to be around people, I listened as the pastor explained that Jesus was friends with sinners. Immediately recognizing myself as part of that group, I laughed. I continued listening, though, as the preacher gave examples of people Jesus embraced—adulterers, tax collectors, and people of different cultural groups that Jesus was supposed to hate. So I decided to have an open mind.

And I thought, *Wow, it's pretty cool that the preacher gets up there and gets to speak to and influence all these people. I wonder if I can do that one day.* I met the preacher afterward and introduced myself. When he asked more about me, I told him about the spoken-word poetry I had been doing at the time. The spoken word was how I expressed myself and described the different situations I found myself in. The pastor asked for my phone number, and we went our separate ways.

A few months later, toward the end of January, the pastor called me and asked if I could prepare a three-minute spoken-word piece for black history month. Extremely excited, I edited a piece I had been doing titled "Throwback," which highlighted remembering our black ancestors.

The church had me perform this piece at three services with a combined attendance of over ten thousand. It was the first time I had ever spoken in front of a large audience. I remember rubbing my sweaty, nervous palms on my black jeans while I breathed rhythmically just before I stood in front of everyone. I barely remember the spoken word, all I remember was what came after: a standing ovation. After all three services, I got a standing ovation. But, greater than that, I got acceptance. It felt like home. It was the family of God.

Here's the poem:

The word throwback goes further back
Than the seats in the "lack"
Streets and crack,
Jerseys and hats,
The word throwback is something like those old graves
Like those old slaves who paved the way for us,
Worked hard day to day for us
I'm telling you it took somebody,
That took somebody, that took somebody,
For us to be here today
For me being Black standing here proud today
Throwback with me,
Throwback and hear thee,
Slaves from the olden days
Before my time talk.
"Isaac, masta says wees besta have dat cotton field picked
       clean. He sayses wintas almost here."
"Isaac!"
"Isaac, wakes up, Isaac!"
"I's hears ya, May. I just cants works todays now my neck
       and back done hurt too!"
I mean, my ancestors should've had cribs on MTV.
A few flat screens, and a song on V-103
Talking about their necks and backs
All the beatings they took and hard work they put in
Just to get us here, and now that we are here we consider
       the word throwback as jerseys and hats
Throwback jerseys and hats
N'all, let's throwback to

Malcom X and Martin Luther King
Lift every voice and sing or Rosa Parks
Saying, "I'm tired, I'm not giving up my seat!"
Or all those great
Black inventors that everyone keeps forgetting
    to mention
Giving no recognition, who probably invented the seats
    we sit in, or the beds we sleep in
You know,
To me
Throwback is black
Because black is bold
Black is beautiful
Black is smart
Black is everything,
Black is even what color my eye turned after one fight.
Now, no disrespect to my Caucasian, Hispanic, and
    Asian brothers
Y'all are still on my care list
But just put in your notes, Blacks has had a prayer list, a
    longer share list, a four-hundred-year-old slave ditch,
    a curse from Satan
Millions of Black mothers with no fathers for babies, a
    lot of Section 8 lists, and lot of Blacks on the crime
    incarcerated list and the list goes on goes on
On and on
Remember this throwback song
"We Shall Overcome"
Well, freedom has rung
In a sense
If we help each other out and stop competing,

I said, "Freedom has rung in a sense if we help each other
    out and stop competing."
Now,
To me throwback is being real to self, and never
    forgetting where self comes from because self has
    no price tag and that's throwback![3]

It was a strange feeling at first, everyone standing up and clapping for someone like me. It was my first attempt to connect with both my history and community at the same time. Just a few months before, I was getting high and drunk on Saturday nights, and here I was on stage using my spoken word to share my deepest pains and struggles. These people stood up and accepted me anyway. The community embraced who I was, what I struggled with, and where I came from. This was life changing for me.

I got down from the stage afterward and people told me things like, "You're going places. You have such an amazing gift of communicating. You've got to share your gift with other young people." And for the first time in my life I was being supported and affirmed by a community for skills I had. I was told that I had something to offer that was valuable and that my pain could be used positively for reaching people. Suddenly, the community I found helped me discover my purpose.

In this community there were people who helped me find jobs and get through college. One mentor even lent me his truck for an entire year so I could get back and forth to school. These people showed me that I was valuable and worth investing in. By surrounding myself with these people, I started to believe them.

I think we're responsible for being in and growing communities. The good communities we find are the powerful ones that help launch us into who we want to be. Of course, some communities have the power to do the opposite as well. It's up to us to find and participate in communities that propel us forward.

Community we create. When first tasked with writing about community, I was conflicted. For most of my life, I felt I didn't belong. *Misfit* is a word I refer to often. Growing up I played a lot of sports. It was something we did in the community where I was raised. I also wrote a lot of poetry. But I didn't tell many people that I wrote poetry until I was much older: it was viewed as feminine (the last thing a young boy wants to be called by his friends). I spent a lot of time on the streets thinking about the world's big concepts but never shared my thoughts for fear of sounding like an outsider.

Those feelings continued in almost everything I pursued. The church was a safe place, but some of my views sounded a bit radical for most of the environments surrounding me. In many settings, I felt as though I didn't fit into the traditional church and was told by church people it was because the way I was running the ministry didn't "fit" what they were doing. I started a nonprofit and began to create a community of misfits.

We're always afraid to be ourselves until we find other people who are like us. We use being a misfit to engage in relationships with people who are misfits as well. Only after having felt that pain deeply can we understand someone who is excluded from society. This is how I connect to the poor, the voiceless, and those who feel socially isolated. I know how it feels to be alone, and I imagine you do too. I imagine you have more in common with someone living on the streets than you think.

My friend Dave Gibbons wrote a book called *Xealots* in which he talks about how our pain is often viewed as an abnormality when it can be used as our superpower. This comes in handy when we're building communities with people who, at first glance, might not appear to have much in common with us. Embracing our pain and the thing that drives us to create something beautiful in the world becomes our guide to connect with those around us.

I think Jesus was a misfit too. We often hear stories of how he'd go into synagogues or the temple and flip tables and challenge the widely accepted thinking. He was considered an extremist because he hung with sinners instead of religious leaders. He hung out with people who, in many ways, looked like you and me. This was the embodied practice of his whole life.

When I was screening our documentary *Voiceless*, I traveled to a small town near a Mennonite community. When we finished screening the documentary, we took a walk through the community. The whole town looked like it was straight out of *Little House on the Prairie*. We approached a woman, Dawn, who told us they accepted all people here. She went on, "If we meet a homeless person, we'll invite them for dinner, give them space, clothes, whatever we have that's extra."

"Wow," someone from our group said, "that's a lot. Why would you do that?"

Her simple response, "Well, that's what Jesus would do."

She's right, of course. As Christians we quote Bible verses like Hebrews 2:10, "Everything belongs to God, and all things were created by his power" (CEV). Theologically, we say we believe that everything comes from God and is God's, but I wonder if we live a little differently.

What if we approached the community around us without being attached to our belongings? Why does living like Jesus still sound so radical?

Last month I spoke to a nonprofit leader and friend about the reality that there are enough beds in houses throughout the United States to provide a space for everyone in our communities. When people hear this they often respond with surprise, "Well, we couldn't just let homeless people into our houses. It's not safe. What if they take something?" But we use Airbnb and let strangers stay in our homes, and we also stay in the homes of strangers. Why does it sound strange when the purpose is to provide help instead?

In opposition to our fears and doubts, I wonder if the better next question is, Would Jesus do it anyway? I've got a feeling he would, but I'll let you take it up with him.

I know firsthand that a community has the power to change the trajectory of a life. It works both ways—negatively and positively. Yet I know for sure that no positive change is made by one person forever alone. We're just not made to live like that. Dr. King said, "An individual has not started living until he can rise above the narrow confines of his individualistic concerns to the broader concerns of all humanity."[4]

So how can we empower those experiencing homelessness or poverty to make that change? It goes back to the idea of a global village. Maybe Jesus got that concept because he knew what it looked like to see us as one created family from the very beginning.

As for creating these types of communities, two things are certain: (1) you must be patient, and (2) you must be willing to get hurt.

Be patient with people in your community. In most cases, they've been in other communities doing the same things every day for years. You can't meet them and expect them to change over a weekend. Patterns take longer to unravel than that, and huge life change is messy. In his book *Love Does*, Bob Goff says, "I used to want to fix people, but now I just want to be with them."[5]

And it's okay to get hurt. We're never immune to this sort of pain, and most certainly not when we're trying to cultivate deep communities that change what people believe they can do with their lives. I've been hurt doing this work, of course. But I've been hurt even more by people in the church. We're all human.

In the end, creating communities is simple. When you love people, you help them find food and shelter, and then you empower them to be all they can be. We have the power to choose which communities we will embrace and which we will create.

CHAPTER TEN

CREATING CONSISTENT RHYTHMS

People are always more generous during the holiday season. From my work in the nonprofit and church sectors, I've seen a lot of this sort of cyclical giving spirit. All nonprofits know the hustle of the last quarter to make big asks, hold fundraisers, and reach out to donors.

A few years ago during the holiday season, a group from a local church reached out to me and with extreme excitement told us, "We want to raise money for toys for kids who won't get Christmas presents this year!"

"All right," I said, "There are some kids in the community that we could . . ."

"Oh, great," the woman responded, "we're going to think and pray about which toy we can give and we'll start raising the money."

"Okay," I said.

"Great, we'll be in touch!" and in her eagerness, she hung up.

A few weeks later I got an email from the same group with the news that the project was fully funded and that they decided to fundraise enough to buy bikes for fifty poor kids. And that they'd like to organize a big giveaway reveal for all the kids who would be getting the brand new bikes.

As I read the email I dropped my head and sighed. While their eagerness to give was a good and beautiful thing—much was missing from this encounter.

They didn't realize that many of the young children in the community didn't know how to ride a bike. Many of their fathers were in prison because of what Michelle Alexander has called the New Jim Crow (dealing with the mass incarceration complex). Thus these kids were being raised by other family members who often didn't have the time or resources to teach these kids how to ride a bike. Was gifting fifty kids from the "hood" brand new bikes really the way to cultivate positive change and growth within a community?

At the same time, I could feel the excitement from the church group who thought they were doing this amazing thing. I can imagine the leader getting up every Sunday for the previous month during announcements to tell the congregation, "Hey! We're raising money to give underprivileged kids bikes. Let's fill this chart and see if we can hit our goal of fifty bikes. Sponsor a kid today!"

Where many of us go wrong isn't in the "we want to do this nice thing for someone else" idea, it's the mentality behind the event, what I call a "checklist mentality." This mentality is developed over years of doing what we've always seen done: hold more canned food drives, fill more boxes with gas station gifts, donate more clothes for the poor.

The intentions are good, but these sorts of events are often not so helpful to the people they're supposed to serve. Instead, it helps us check off a box on our list of "good Christian things to do." Jesus said to serve the poor; I donated a bike—check.

We're missing the depth that could create lasting change in a community. We trade it for something that makes us feel nice and sounds good during Sunday-morning announcements.

When we don't look for or create depth in these encounters, we perpetuate a cycle that makes transformation even more difficult. These dynamics lead to unhealthy relationships in which one side tells the other what they want or need. There's no empowerment or dignity, and no trusting relationships are created.

The checklist mentality isn't able to communicate Jesus' ultimate message: you are loved, valued, and seen. Instead, it communicates: you lack much; I have more; here's something you don't need or know how to use.

What is the alternative?

In the case at hand, it would have been good for the people of this church to ask what this community lacks or to spend time with the kids before buying them something. How can we show these kids that they're loved and seen? What does it require us to commit to? It's necessary to have a learning posture and listen to community members rather than coming in as outsiders with our own agendas.

In the same way that any healthy relationship develops, it takes time, commitment, and being willing to show up again and again. Instead of approaching these types of encounters with checklists and events, we have to shift our mindset to cultivate relationships through rhythms. Sustainable impact happens when we cultivate consistent rhythms.

When we begin to see ourselves and others as inextricably linked to the point where their pains ail us, then the cycle of coming with an event mentality will begin to change. To view people experiencing poverty as brothers, sisters, and friends rather than as checklist items is pivotal in this journey.

THE RHYTHMIC COSMOS

Genesis 1:1-2 says, "In the beginning, God created the heavens and earth. Now the earth was formless and empty, darkness was over the surface of the deep, and the Spirit of God was hovering over the waters."

Out of darkness, God created light and dark, day and night, sun and moon. Each created thing belonged to a time and place and had a specific rhythm. God also created rhythms, patterns, and systems as an important and healthy part of our lives.

Ecclesiastes 3:1 mentions rhythms and seasons as well, "There is a time for everything, and a season for every activity under the heavens." Even Jesus operated out of these sorts of rhythms. He had moments when he spoke to large crowds, rested, prayed, and spent time with his disciples.

If those experiencing injustice and inequality are important to us, how then will we make them a rhythm in our lives? What rhythms do we already have?

In my life, rhythms are the reason for almost everything I've accomplished. Every twelve months I create a "growth plan." In it I plan for what I want to learn, how I want to grow, where I want to serve, and what I want to accomplish in the next twelve months. I look at the plan and then decide which rhythms I need to integrate into my daily life (or which rhythms I need to take out) to make my goals possible.

What rhythms do you have in your life? Wake up, drink coffee, go to work, come home, watch TV, spend time with family? Do you bowl on Tuesday nights? How about a date night with your spouse?

Adding rhythms into an already busy life feels hard, but our rhythms reflect our core values. If something is important, we make time for it. These rhythms can't be added because of guilt or through behavior modification but only from a transformed heart. When we operate by and add these out of guilt, we fall back into the checklist mindset and risk growing bitter. Instead, we incorporate these rhythms into a lifestyle of service.

There is a certain balance we must find for our internal and external growth. Many of us may recognize the rhythms needed for our own personal growth, which is important. But we often overlook how external service changes us. As we're constantly focused on self-care, self-help, and personal growth, we can easily turn inward and become self-focused. To turn our focus outward, we need external rhythms of service in which our sole focus is on others. On the other hand, community activists and leaders are prone to the opposite. We can be so focused on outward service that we can neglect our personal lives and families, ending in burnout.

Rhythms are the easiest way to find the balance. Continually balancing ourselves and our lives is how we refuel ourselves and move toward a healthy spiritual life.

A LIFESTYLE OF SERVICE

We may need to redefine what *service* means. One summer day, my daughter, Zion, came into my room and said, "Hey, Dad. I want to go to work with you tomorrow." She knows that my work is running a community nonprofit center.

Intrigued, I asked, "Wouldn't you rather be at home watching cartoons, playing outside, or playing video games? Doing something fun?"

"Going to work with you is fun to me. Helping people is fun," she said.

Her sentiment surprised me. Then I was surprised that I was surprised by her statement. It's pretty cool to think that my daughter believes it's fun to pack grocery bags, organize closets, and clean a bus that has a barbershop in it. Maybe it's because she has seen what it means to a family that has no food or to a child her age who gets clothes. Whatever the case, it's been fun to see how God has allowed her to connect her faith to being active and consistent. She's only ten; I can't wait to see what she'll do when she gets older.

I have a couple of questions, though. Why don't we think that service, being around other people, and helping people is fun? How can we redefine these routines and activities so they fit into our lives and aren't seen as a burden?

We must stop putting so much pressure on these encounters as the ultimate, most meaningful moments in their lives. We get to have these interactions with people as often as we'd like. By stopping long enough to engage, we are able to see value in others that we trained ourselves to miss before. In most cases, when we make service a routine, the people we come in contact with will give us much more than we could ever think or imagine.

A few weeks ago a volunteer came by for the first time in a while, and I asked her where she'd been. She told me she had been swamped with schedules, running around, and trying to manage work and her personal life. She felt like she had hit a brick wall. All of this had drained her, so she stopped everything she was doing and decided to serve and be around people.

We were helping people with groceries that day, and for a few minutes I watched her get into a conversation with a woman, but I was pulled away to assist with something else before I got to see how it turned out. A few hours later the volunteer told me about the encounter she had with the woman. They had talked about faith, and the woman in line prayed for the volunteer.

The volunteer, who had a steady job, supportive family, and drove to our center in her nice car, burst into tears as she told us how much it meant to her to have someone see her and pray for her. None of the external things she came with determined her true wealth. I'm lucky enough to see these moments every day. Real relationships are being cultivated by people willing to show up.

These sorts of conversations don't often happen without getting to know someone first. No one shares their entire life story, pains, and burdens the first time they meet someone. Trust takes time to develop. Relationships and change take consistency and dependency, which can lead to real cyclical transformation.

ONE AT A TIME

As we develop consistency and dream of changing the cycle, we begin to believe that we are responsible for a transformation of great magnitude. I often feel this burden too. We exist in a data-driven society where numbers matter. Who has the most followers on social media? How much money do you make? How many bikes did we give away? We want to know the numbers, and we want them to be higher.

In 2016, I walked from Atlanta to Washington, DC, and in 2018 from Atlanta to Memphis. The first journey took over two months to complete; the second took one month. These were radical campaigns that required me to acquire completely new rhythms to walk hundreds of miles. On one hand, it would have been easy to focus on the big, national news I was making. Somehow, though, that wasn't what got me through the miles and miles I had to walk in the heat, rain, and through threatening towns. What helped get me through those places was focusing on the one. Can I reach one person today? Can I help transform one person's life today? Did I help someone take steps to get out of a bad situation?

Focusing on the one keeps me grounded. If it changes or helps one person's life, it's worth it. Jesus did it for the one all the time—for the woman at the well, the disabled man, the dying girl. When he healed the blind man, he told him not to tell anyone about what had happened, but the man told the entire town about his transformation. It's not always about solving the entire world's problems but changing the world for the one person who is in front of us. The consistent things we do by showing up every day can transform the lives of the people around us, if we are willing. There are different ways to minister and help others. Jesus listened to people, he fed people, he cried with sisters, he calmed chaotic situations.

When our nonprofit first started, a woman in her sixties, Marie, served with us every week, and she was one of the bubbliest people I had ever met. Marie had more energy than I did. She consistently came in and helped us while always mentioning that she had a big, mysterious project she was working on. But Marie wouldn't tell us what it was. After a few months, she came in to work with us and walked straight up to me and said, "Okay! I'm about to do it!"

"What are you about to do?" I asked her.

"My big project. I'm about to pay for someone's entire college tuition," Marie told me with a big smile on her face.

Surprised, I asked, "Uh, what?"

"Yeah, I've been putting a little away every time I had a little extra money. Five dollars here. Ten dollars there. Been putting it away for the last forty years. I created an account since I never had any kids, and I let the compound interest add up."

Marie had begun a friendship with a young man who wasn't sure how he was going to pay for college, and she knew that this was the kid she had been saving up for. This is an example of the impact of one but also how small things over time can make a huge difference.

If people were to sum up your life in one sentence, what would they say about you?

Where do you spend your resources? What type of legacy will you leave? What would you give your life to if you were going to die in thirty days? Are you happy with the rhythms you've created in your life?

God has given you one life. It's shorter than you both know or can imagine. Many of us say we want to make changes and do things differently once we get to a certain place in life, but all we have is what we add up day after day. Your daily rhythms and consistent practices determine the type of life you're going to live and the impact you'll make. Think about where you want to go, and be honest with yourself about how you're going to get there.

Jesus said the way to the greatness is through service: "Whoever wants to become great among you must be your servant" (Matthew 20:26).

CONCLUSION

EACH ONE MATTERS

On my first night living under an underpass, Robert and I talked about why I had decided to come out to stay with others living there, and he asked me, "You know, a lot of people come out here and bring stuff like soap and clothes, but why'd you really come out here and stay?"

"I wanted to know what it was really like. How could I help if I didn't know how it actually felt to sleep outside on the cold ground or in a tent in the pouring rain?" I responded.

After a few hours of getting to know each other, he shared his story and what led him to his life on the streets. He said he had been living on the streets since he was a teenager. His mom was addicted to crack and even gave him some as a young teen. His father wasn't around, so Robert raised himself. He was in and out of jail in his twenties, ending up on the streets at thirty-three, addicted to the same drug his mom gave him while he was growing up.

Sure, he might have made some bad decisions that landed him in jail, but I also wondered whether he ever had significant opportunities to make better choices. Did he ever see or have an example of what it would look like for someone like him to choose a different life? Probably not.

What does that mean for us? It reminds me of what it was like to find hope in Jesus. By God's grace, someone showed me what it would look like for someone like me to make that choice and live a different way.

I believe we're made to be in community, especially in relationship with God. When we experience spiritual poverty, when we lack a relationship with God, no possessions, people, or even experiences will fill that gap. Without God, having access to everything in the world will leave us feeling alone and isolated.

I know we can all relate to that sort of poverty. Jesus told a parable about a shepherd and his sheep:

> Suppose one of you has a hundred sheep and loses one of them. Doesn't he leave the ninety-nine in the open country and go after the lost sheep until he finds it? And when he finds it, he joyfully puts it on his shoulders and goes home. Then he calls his friends and neighbors together and says, "Rejoice with me; I have found my lost sheep." I tell you that in the same way there will be more rejoicing in heaven over one sinner who repents than over ninety-nine righteous persons who do not need to repent. (Luke 15:4-7)

Our natural instinct is to wonder, *Why in the world would you go after one when you have ninety-nine other safe sheep?* Maybe it's the math that doesn't seem to make sense to me, or the business part of my brain says, *Count that one as a loss. Your time is better used fostering and caring for the ninety-nine.* Luckily, God doesn't think like that. If he did, we would be out of luck.

The shepherd knew the ninety-nine were safe and went after the one, which illustrates that God doesn't care for some but for all—even the one who has wandered away or made bad choices or is sleeping under a bridge or in a penthouse. There are no stipulations. God leaves the safe and pursues those in unsafe situations, even when leaving the ninety-nine is uncomfortable and it takes some work to find the one person. There is great value in reaching the one.

We must always be on the lookout for the one who is poor in spirit, who is vulnerable, who is oppressed. Our connection to the one is that we were once that one. We were in need of rescuing. If we truly understand that we once were the one, that should then compel us to go out and be the bridge for someone else.

In the world, one person is not viewed as important. Worldwide, over three billion people live in poverty, living on less than $2.50 a day. How would we ever make a difference in the lives of three billion? It's hard for us to even begin to wrap our minds around this number. We may not have that opportunity, but we do have the opportunity to make a difference every time we see one person. That one is someone Jesus died for. Are we willing to live like that?

The one often seems inconvenient too. Why leave the ninety-nine in a place of safety and comfort to seek out ways to bring the one back into the fold? It could be a lot of work. God never looks at the amount of work though; the amount of work always pales in comparison to the person's worth.

One in our society isn't celebrated. Can you imagine people at your church getting up on Sunday morning announcements and saying that they raised enough money for one bike or to feed one family? It doesn't sound the same as a great, big, double- or triple-digit number. But in the last verse of the parable, Jesus says, "There will be more rejoicing in heaven over one sinner who repents than over ninety-nine righteous persons who do not need to repent." We've got to celebrate every single one.

I wonder what it would look like if every church, every person who claims to love Jesus, adopted the *one* mentality. There are certainly enough Christians in my home city of Atlanta for each to care for one homeless person, one foster child, or one family struggling with poverty. If we took the same approach as Jesus, we could have a dramatic impact on our communities.

IMPACT OVER PERFECTION

I often say to a good friend, "Impact over perfection." It's a reminder that most things don't need to be perfect; it's more important that they make an impact.

Perfection in solving the problem can be a disease that causes us to remain in our comfort zones or become so paralyzed we never take a step further. Just focus on the impact. The delivery doesn't have to be—and never will be—perfect.

That's why it's hard to develop an exact solution to systemic poverty. Honestly, I think it's always going to be messy. One day will be different from the rest, and every person will need different kinds of support. What won't change is our focus to treat everyone with Jesus' love and have an open mind to hear their stories.

If we become too focused on the perfect formula or solution, we'll miss the point and won't be able to help the people we're serving. Changing the lives of the people around us happens organically because we put ourselves out there and admit we aren't doing it perfectly. (Who relates to perfect people anyway?)

In my early twenties, I spent a lot of time writing. I wrote a lot about my childhood and teens, especially about the decisions I made and why I determined to start making better ones. I compiled all my writings and produced a self-published book called *U-Turn*.

One weekend I was asked to speak to a group at a youth detention center where I had been a resident years before. I remember looking at the young people's faces, sitting in the chairs I once sat in, and it was as if I was given the chance to give my younger self advice.

I told them about my struggles, my relationships with family, and even my relationship with God. When I finished speaking, I had the opportunity to talk to and pray for the kids, who were given a copy of my book. That night I was sitting in my living room and my phone rang multiple times from a number I didn't recognize.

I picked it up and a young woman on the other end told me she was from the youth detention center where I had just spoken. She had snuck out, found a phone, and called my number from the back of my book. She told me that she was sixteen, was about to be transferred to an adult facility, and was facing fifteen years in prison for being in the company of people who had committed a crime. She was guilty by association.

"I don't know what I'm going to do," she told me. I told her about a time I wasn't sure what I was going to do. I'm wary of giving answers since everyone's lives are different, but I wanted her to know that she wasn't alone and that I had been in her shoes. I told her to call back if she needed to and we hung up.

A few minutes later I got a call from a similar number. "Hello, is this Terence Lester? Did Sarah just call you? I'm her case manager. Thank you so much for answering. Thank you!"

"Of course, I was happy to talk to her. What's going on?" I asked.

"Well, she had told people that if you didn't answer the phone, she was going to kill herself in the detention center."

That story gives me chills. I never imagined I could be that crucial for someone. All because I shared my story in a book, put my number in the back, and answered the phone when it rang.

I didn't do anything extremely significant or have a perfect conversation, but somehow I changed her life. I saw myself in her. The broken, messed up, lonely, and confused parts of me were in her too.

I think when we see our similarities with one another, we're able to identify with our common bonds of pain and lack to see that we're looking for someone to fill the gap. Some days you and I are lucky enough to be that person. Other times we're able to bring someone to someone or something that fills the need.

So now, you have the chance to decide who you'll see and what you'll do with the people you encounter. Some people will be poor in spirit and some poor in a physical sense—sometimes both. There will be times when that person will be you. If we decide together that we're going to love like Jesus and give all we have to the one, I can promise that you and the people around you will be better for it.

Put yourself in someone else's shoes. Find out what they need. Tell them you see them. Show them you're there. Tell the broken, weary, poor, and lonely that they're not alone. Start the soup kitchen. Write the book. Speak in a prison. Volunteer more than normal. Feed the homeless. Pick up trash. Advocate for those caught in sex trafficking. Do something, anything for the one.

It will cost you nothing but will change the world for everyone, if you learn to see. See people no matter where they are, who they are, or what they're doing. It can be as simple as picking up the phone and telling someone they're not alone. When I was able to show Sarah she was seen over the phone that day, her life was changed and so was mine. See people. Show people you see them. Look them in the eyes and let them know they are seen.

You are loved. You are known. You are seen.

Go see people.

ACKNOWLEDGMENTS

I love to read a famous quote when reflecting on the wonderful people who have made it possible for me to do certain things and have helped me along the way. The following quote is attributed to the well-known mathematician Isaac Newton. I'm pretty sure he knew what it meant to count the cost. Although the quote is brief, the words speak to the fact that we have better views, better advantages, and see things more clearly because of the sacrifice and support of others. He said, "If I have seen further it is by standing on the shoulders of giants." We all see better and experience more in life because of the people who paved the way for us long before we were thought about and because of those who supported us along the way.

With that being said, I would like to especially thank those people who have supported me along the way, encouraged me, and even sacrificed their time so I could somehow see further.

To my wife, Cecilia Lester: Honestly, without your loving support and encouragement, I wouldn't be able to do the work that our family does. You are my rock. I would also like to thank and acknowledge my children with similar admiration, Zion Joy and Terence II. Thank you for being amazing children and for telling me to keep helping people because you think that's cool.

Special thanks go to my mother, Dr. Connie Walker, for never giving up on me, and to my sister, Ashley Lester, and her son Carmelo, and my father, Tyrone Lester, whose relationship I have come to value and thank God for. I'm thankful God restored our relationship. Thank you also to my stepfather, Dewitt Walker Sr., for always encouraging me to pursue a life of service.

To my book agent, Tawny Johnson: Thank you for having the vision for this book from day one and believing it would one day make it into the hands of people and push them to love and see those who are invisible.

To my editor, Al Hsu: Thank you for being such great support along the way. Thank you for seeing potential in this book and making it the best it could be.

To the whole IVP family: Thank you for welcoming me with open arms and believing that my voice and story matters.

Kellie McGann helped me to think through and process ideas found on these pages. My wife and I thank you for your labor of love and support on this journey.

To one of my closest friends, Harvey Strickland: Thank you for walking with me since day one and always believing that this would happen. To my friend Mike Fye, who has become a brother, thank you for helping us to lead strong. Additionally, I want to give a special thanks to Johnny Taylor and Ali Brathwaite for supporting two of my most important campaigns that helped to change many false perceptions about the poor. I appreciate you being friends in my life. Thank you to James Brookshire, who walked with me to Memphis in 2018 to display unity and provide support, and to his wife Shannon, who allowed him to take off work to do it. Thank you to my assistant, Julia Webb, and her husband, Michael Webb, for faithfully praying for this book throughout the entire process.

To the Love Beyond Walls team: I'm thankful for every volunteer who has ever served and all those who have supported our advocacy work over the years.

Thank you to my friend Dave Gibbons for encouraging me, being one of my mentors, and writing the foreword to this book. Thank you for pushing me to lead strong and be a "xealot." Thank you to Jeff Shinabarger of Plywood People for creating a special place for social entrepreneurs—where people like myself can dream and get permission and try crazy ideas like the ones I've done.

Last, I'd like to say a special thank you to a few guys who have poured into my life over the last eight years: Pastor Brian Bloye, Mac Lake, Kevin Dunlap, and A. J. McMichael. I don't think I'd be the leader I am today with your personal investment in me.

Thank you all for supporting me and allowing me to stand on the shoulders of giants.

QUESTIONS FOR REFLECTION AND DISCUSSION

INTRODUCTION: SEARCHING FOR HOME

1. Have you ever felt like an outcast? When and where?
2. What does home mean to you? How do you define home?
3. What does the good news mean for the outsider?
4. How do you define poverty?
5. What does poverty look like in the world today?
6. Where did your beliefs about the poor come from?
7. In what ways does spiritual poverty relate to people who are materially poor?

CHAPTER 1: DEMYSTIFYING POVERTY

1. Have you ever felt excluded? What did it feel like?
2. Why do you think people who are homeless are excluded today?
3. How does God feel about the mistreatment of people who are homeless and poor?
4. Have you ever asked a person dealing with homelessness or poverty what it takes to make it through the day? If so, what did the person say?
5. What does it take to escape poverty?

CHAPTER 2: YOU DON'T HAVE TO FEAR

1. What does 2 Corinthians 8:9 mean to you?

2. Why do you think people fear the poor?

3. Why do people feel great emotion when observing someone in need?

4. Why do we fear people we do not know?

5. How do we measure worth in today's society?

6. What is the source of worth?

7. In what ways have you feared the poor? Are you willing to face those fears?

8. Do you believe class has separated people in modern society? If so, how and why?

9. How might Jesus have us care for the poor and overlooked?

CHAPTER 3: MAKING ROOM IN THE MARGINS

1. We all have too much on our plates. What on your plate needs to be removed?

2. Why do we glorify busyness in our culture?

3. What could you do more of to help others?

4. What might happen if we spent our time building up people instead of building bigger storehouses for all our possessions?

5. How would the world change if we made room in our margins for the vulnerable, marginalized, and voiceless?

CHAPTER 4: HOW MUCH IS ENOUGH?

1. When have you felt like you had more than enough?

2. What do you do with your excess items?

3. How could they be used to help someone else?

4. Do you think everyone is responsible for the poor? If not, who is?

5. Do you think God wants all of us to address the issue of poverty? If so, why?

6. How does greed keep us from helping the poor?

CHAPTER 5: IGNORANCE CAN BE HURTFUL

1. How is ignorance harmful?

2. Have you been ignorant about something and subsequently hurt someone? Did you apologize?

3. Do you think God calls us to tackle our blind spots? If so, how do we do this?

4. How can we challenge our ignorance and be more loving as Christ was?

CHAPTER 6: YOU ARE PART OF THE SOLUTION

1. Identify three ways you can make a difference in the world.

2. Have you taken a spiritual gifts inventory to see what gifts you have that could be used by God?

3. How could you use your gifts to help those who are poor?

4. Name a few people who inspire you to live courageously.

CHAPTER 7: DIFFERENT COMMUNITIES, DIFFERENT NEEDS

1. When you have been in a community or place different from your own, what did you learn? What did you take away from this experience?

2. What did you wish you had known before you entered that community?

3. How do you think we isolate ourselves based on misunderstandings about different communities?

4. Why is diversity important to God?

5. Should Christians learn cultural diversity techniques? Why?

6. Can a lack of experience with diversity keep us from helping those who need help? Why?

7. How can we help those who have mental health issues?

8. What are you doing to equip yourself to come alongside these persons?

CHAPTER 8: DIGNITY AND HOW TO SEE PEOPLE

1. Why do you think it's hard to affirm the dignity of the poor?

2. Have you ever overlooked the poor? Why?

3. How do you think Jesus would affirm those who are overlooked?

4. What does the word *dignity* mean to you? Where does human dignity come from?

5. How can we ensure that the poor know they are worthy and have dignity?

6. How does bias hinder people from hearing the good news?

7. What would you do if you felt you didn't belong or were not welcomed?

8. How do you think the poor and homeless feel when they are not welcomed?

CHAPTER 9: CREATING COMMUNITIES

1. How could healthy community change someone's life?

2. Why is community important to God?

3. How has community changed your life?

4. Why is it hard for people who are poor or homeless to be invited into a community?

5. What can you do to create community with people who are not like you?

CHAPTER 10: CREATING CONSISTENT RHYTHMS

1. Why do people tend to resist serving others?

2. What stands in the way of service becoming part of your lifestyle?

3. How can you make serving others a normal part of your life?

4. Why don't we think service is fun or enjoyable?

5. What should be done to ensure we are not creating a check-box mentality?

6. Why should we strive to enhance the relational aspect of service?

CONCLUSION: EACH ONE MATTERS

1. What does it mean to seek "the one" Jesus talked about in Luke 15?

2. Why is the one important?

3. Have you ever felt like the one? What was that experience like?

4. How can you start seeing people and going after the one?

5. How can you make an outsider feel like the one who God seeks to provide love and grace?

6. Where will you start after reading this book?

NOTES

INTRODUCTION: SEARCHING FOR HOME

[1]Joseph R. Myers, *The Search to Belong: Rethinking Intimacy, Community, and Small Groups* (Grand Rapids: Zondervan, 2003).

[2]Howard Thurman, *Jesus and the Disinherited* (Boston: Beacon Press, 1996), 13.

[3]Barbara Ehrenreich, quoted in Tavis Smiley and Cornel West, *The Rich and the Rest of Us* (Philadelphia: Free Library of Philadelphia, 2012), 22.

[4]Martin Luther King Jr., "Dr. Martin Luther King's Visit to Cornell College," Cornell College News Center, accessed January 26, 2019, https://news .cornellcollege.edu/dr-martin-luther-kings-visit-to-cornell-college. King delivered his address October 15, 1962.

1 DEMYSTIFYING POVERTY

[1]David Gaider, "David Gaider Quotes," *AZ Quotes*, accessed January 26, 2019, www.azquotes.com/quote/672800.

[2]Eleanor Krause and Isabel V. Sawhill, "Seven Reasons to Worry About the American Middle Class," Brookings Institution, June 5, 2018, www .brookings.edu/blog/social-mobility-memos/2018/06/05/seven-reasons-to -worry-about-the-american-middle-class.

[3]Jill Rosen, "Study: Children's Life Trajectories Largely Determined by Family They Are Born Into," *Hub*, June 2, 2014, https://hub.jhu.edu /2014/06/02/karl-alexander-long-shadow-research.

[4]Chad W. Dunn, quoted in Sari Horwitz, "Getting a Photo ID so You Can Vote Is Easy. Unless You're Poor, Black, Latino or Elderly," *Washington Post*, May 23, 2016, www.washingtonpost.com/politics/courts_law/getting-a -photo-id-so-you-can-vote-is-easy-unless-youre-poor-black-latino-or

-elderly/2016/05/23/8d5474ec-20f0-11e6-8690-f14ca9de2972_story
.html?utm_term=.f53fbcb44885.

[5]Arthur Dobrin, "The Effects of Poverty on the Brain," *Am I Right?* (blog),
Psychology Today, October 22, 2012, www.psychologytoday.com/us/blog/am
-i-right/201210/the-effects-poverty-the-brain.

[6]Gillian B. White, "Escaping Poverty Requires Almost 20 Years with Nearly
Nothing Going Wrong," *Atlantic*, April 2017, www.theatlantic.com
/business/archive/2017/04/economic-inequality/524610.

2 YOU DON'T HAVE TO FEAR

[1]"Imago Dei ('image of God')," *PBS*, accessed January 2, 2019, www.pbs.org
/faithandreason/theogloss/imago-body.html.

[2]"Statistics & Facts on the U.S. Cosmetics and Makeup Industry," *Statistic
Portal*, www.statista.com/topics/1008/cosmetics-industry.

[3]Mother Teresa, "Quotable Quote," *Goodreads*, accessed January 26,
2019, www.goodreads.com/quotes/71796-being-unwanted-unloved
-uncared-for-forgotten-by-everybody-i-think.

[4]Much of the rest of this section is lightly adapted from "The Poor People's
Manifesto," *Love Beyond Walls*, April 11, 2018, www.lovebeyondwalls.org
/the-poor-peoples-manifesto.

[5]Robert Bird and Frank Newport, "What Determines How Americans
Perceive Their Social Class?" *Gallup*, February 27, 2017, https://news.gallup
.com/opinion/polling-matters/204497/determines-americans-perceive
-social-class.aspx.

[6]"What Is India's Caste System?" *BBC News*, July 20, 2017, www.bbc.com
/news/world-asia-india-35650616.

[7]Jessica McBurney, "Capitalism," *CommonLit*, 2016, www.commonlit.org
/texts/capitalism.

[8]To see how the prison system and health care have exploited poor people
for profit, see Michelle Alexander, *The New Jim Crow: Mass Incarceration in
the Age of Colorblindness* (New York: New Press, 2012), 215; Michelle
Alexander, "The New Jim Crow," *Course Hero*, accessed January 26, 2019,
www.coursehero.com/lit/The-New-Jim-Crow/introduction-summary; and
Dominique Gilliard, *Rethinking Incarceration: Advocating for Justice That
Restores* (Downers Grove, IL: InterVarsity Press, 2018), 44.

[9]W. Bruce Walsh, Paul J. Hartung, and Mark L. Savickas, *Handbook of Vocational Psychology: Theory, Research, and Practice*, 4th ed. (London: Routledge, 2013), chap. 4.

[10]"Horatio Alger," *Wikipedia*, accessed January 2, 2019, https://en.wikipedia .org/wiki/Horatio_Alger.

[11]Gretchen Frazee, "The Minimum Wage Is Increasing in These 21 States," *PBS News Hour*, January 1, 2019, www.pbs.org/newshour/economy/the -minimum-wage-is-increasing-in-these-21-states.

[12]Howard Thurman, *Jesus and the Disinherited* (Boston: Beacon Press, 1996), 2.

[13]"No Safe Street: A Survey of Hate Crimes and Violence Committed Against Homeless People in 2014 & 2015," National Coalition for the Homeless, July 2016, https://nationalhomeless.org/wp-content/uploads /2016/07/HCR-2014-151.pdf.

[14]"2 Charged in Taped Attack on NJ Homeless Man." *NBC New York*, December 20, 2011, www.nbcnewyork.com/news/local/Homeless-Man -Attack-Video-Tape-NJ-Wall-Township-135886238.html.

[15]"L.A. Man Arrested, Accused of Setting Homeless Woman on Fire as She Slept on Van Nuys Bus Bench," *Daily News*, August 28, 2017, www .dailynews.com/2012/12/27/la-man-arrested-accused-of-setting-homeless -woman-on-fire-as-she-slept-on-van-nuys-bus-bench.

[16]Eleanor Goldberg, "Attacks on the Homeless Jumped 23 Percent Last Year: Report," *Huffington Post*, March 31, 2014, www.huffingtonpost.com /2014/03/31/homeless-attacks_n_5063662.html.

[17]Love Beyond Walls is an organization my wife and I started in 2013 to bring attention to the plight of homelessness and poverty while at the same time mobilizing people to care for those who are poor. In essence, Love Beyond Walls was created as a hopeful response to a society building higher and higher walls. We focus on telling the stories of and working with those wrestling with poverty and homelessness. As an organization, we believe that tangible love overcomes these barriers.

[18]Crystal Ayres, "How Poverty Increases Crime Rates," *Vittana*, January 15, 2017, vittana.org/how-poverty-influences-crime-rates.

[19]Ken Cuccinelli, "Texas Shows How to Reduce Both Incarceration and Crime," *National Review*, May 18, 2015, www.nationalreview.com /2015/05/how-could-we-have-fewer-prisoners-without-more-crime -ask-texas.

3 MAKING ROOM IN THE MARGINS

[1]Richard A. Swenson, *Margin: Restoring Emotional, Physical, Financial, and Time Reserves to Overloaded Lives* (Colorado Springs: NavPress, 2004), 27.

[2]Swenson, *Margin*, 63.

[3]Silvia Bellezza, Neeru Paharia, and Anat Keinan, "Research: Why Americans Are So Impressed by Busyness," *Harvard Business Review*, December 15, 2016, https://hbr.org/2016/12/research-why-americans-are-so-impressed-by-busyness.

[4]"United States of America," *Operation World*, accessed March 22, 2019, http://www.operationworld.org/country/unsa/owtext.html.

4 HOW MUCH IS ENOUGH?

[1]Craig Greenfield, "What Does Jesus Mean, 'The Poor Will Always Be with You'?" *Relevant*, June 29, 2016, https://relevantmagazine.com/reject-apathy/what-does-jesus-mean-poor-will-always-be-you.

[2]David W. Jones, "Was Jesus Rich or Poor—and Why Does It Matter?" *Intersect*, July 7, 2016, http://intersectproject.org/faith-and-economics/jesus-rich-poor-matter.

[3]Henri J. M. Nouwen, "Our Poverty, God's Dwelling Place: August 18," *Henri Nouwen Society*, https://henrinouwen.org/meditation/poverty-gods-dwelling-place/.

[4]Michael Kahn, "Next to Former Peachtree-Pine Shelter, New Residential Tower Announced," *Curbed Atlanta*, January 26, 2018, https://atlanta.curbed.com/atlanta-development/2018/1/26/16935010/peachtree-pine-closed-new-high-rise-apartments.

5 IGNORANCE CAN BE HURTFUL

[1]Northeastern University, "Human Behavior Is 93 Percent Predictable, Research Shows," *Phys.org*, February 23, 2010, phys.org/news/2010-02-human-behavior-percent.html.

[2]Derek Thompson, "Busting the Myth of 'Welfare Makes People Lazy,'" *Atlantic*, March 8, 2018, www.theatlantic.com/business/archive/2018/03/welfare-childhood/555119.

[3]Martha T. S. Laham, "Fastest-Growing Segment of the Homeless Population May Surprise You," *Huffington Post*, June 7, 2017, www.huffpost.com/entry/fastest-growing-segment-of-homeless-population_b_10201782.

[4]"Dignity Museum," *Love Beyond Walls* (blog), September 26, 2018, www .lovebeyondwalls.org/category/love-beyond-walls-story/.

6 YOU ARE PART OF THE SOLUTION

[1]"Black Man Jailed After Trying to Pay Burger King with $10 Bill, Lawsuit Claims," *NBCNews*, May 18, 2018, www.nbcnews.com/news/us -news/homeless-man-jailed-three-months-after-trying-pay-burger -king-n875346.

[2]Michael Eric Dyson, *April 4, 1968: Martin Luther King, Jr.'s Death and How It Changed America* (Philadelphia: Basic Civitas Books, 2008), 9.

[3]Scott W. Allard, "Why Poverty Is Rising Faster in Suburbs Than in Cities," *Conversation*, May 31, 2018, https://theconversation.com/why-poverty-is -rising-faster-in-suburbs-than-in-cities-97155.

7 DIFFERENT COMMUNITIES, DIFFERENT NEEDS

[1]*Voiceless: A Documentary of Systemic Poverty*, Love Beyond Walls, accessed January 7, 2019, https://vimeo.com/222830083.

[2]Jane E. Myers and Thomas J. Sweeney, "The Indivisible Self: An Evidence-Based Model of Wellness," *Journal of Individual Psychology* 60, no. 3 (2004): 234-45, https://libres.uncg.edu/ir/uncg/f/J_Myers_Indivisible _2004.pdf.

[3]Many educational sites use versions of the Wheel of Wellness. This one from Princeton includes a self-assessment tool. See "Wellness Wheel & Assessment," *UMatter*, accessed January 7, 2019, https://umatter.princeton .edu/action-matters/caring-yourself/wellness-wheel-assessment.

8 DIGNITY AND HOW TO SEE PEOPLE

[1]Martin Luther King Jr., *Strength to Love* (New York: Harper & Row, 1963), 37.

[2]Susan Biali, "How to Stop Believing Lies Others Told You About You," *Psychology Today*, September 4, 2012, www.psychologytoday.com/us/blog /prescriptions-life/201209/how-stop-believing-lies-others-told-you -about-you.

9 CREATING COMMUNITIES

[1]Katie Nodjimbadem, "The Racial Segregation of American Cities Was Anything but Accidental," *Smithsonian.com*, May 30, 2017, www .smithsonianmag.com/history/how-federal-government-intentionally -racially-segregated-american-cities-180963494.

[2]George Cronk, "George Herbert Mead (1863-1931)," *Internet Encyclopedia of Philosophy*, accessed January 7, 2019, www.iep.utm.edu/mead.

[3]Terence Lester, "Throwback," 2003. Used by permission.

[4]Martin Luther King Jr., *The Measure of a Man* (Minneapolis: Fortress Press, 2001), 43.

[5]Bob Goff, *Love Does: Discover a Secretly Incredible Life in an Ordinary World* (Nashville: Thomas Nelson, 2012), 1.

ABOUT THE AUTHOR

Terence Lester is the founder and executive director of Love Beyond Walls. He is a community activist, minister, speaker, and author. He believes that all people deserve equity, love, and a chance to change their lives. Terence travels domestically and internationally speaking about issues relating to social justice, poverty, homelessness, faith, and culture. His awareness campaigns on behalf of the poor have been featured in *USA Today*, *Atlanta Journal-Constitution*, *Black Enterprise*, *Rolling Out*, on NBC and Upworthy, and have been viewed by over ten million people globally. His greatest passion involves educating the general public about pressing issues that plague the lives of those who are vulnerable and voiceless and using the educational piece to mobilize an army of people to love and serve those who are unseen. Terence holds four degrees and has written several books. He is happily married to Cecilia, and together they have two wonderful children, Zion Joy and Terence II.

terencelester.com
twitter.com/imterencelester
facebook.com/imterencelester
instagram.com/imterencelester

ABOUT LOVE BEYOND WALLS

Love Beyond Walls is a movement birthed out of the hope that love is greater than walls. One of the most distinguishable characteristics of our organization is our focus on telling the stories of the unseen. We are committed to people that the world passes by because we believe the people struggling with poverty and sleeping on the streets have lives and stories that are just as valuable as ours.

We exist to provide dignity to the homeless and poor by providing a voice, visibility, shelter, community, grooming, and support services to achieve self-sufficiency.

Address: 3270 East Main Street, College Park, GA 30337
Email: info@lovebeyondwalls.org
lovebeyondwalls.org
twitter.com/lovebeyondwalls
facebook.com/lovebeyondwalls
vimeo.com/lovebeyondwalls
instagram.com/lovebeyondwalls